INSPIRATIONS FOR A MOTHER'S SOUL

INSPIRATIONS
for a Mother's Soul

Tyndale House Publishers, Inc.
Wheaton, Illinois

Visit Tyndale's exciting Web site at www.tyndale.com

Questions, notes, and Scripture selection primarily by Rhonda O'Brien

Contributing writers: Jonathan Gray and Shawn A. Harrison

General Editors: V. Gilbert Beers and Ronald A. Beers

Tyndale House Editor: Shawn A. Harrison

Portions of this book compiled from *TouchPoints for Women* and *The TouchPoint Bible,* copyright © 1996 by Tyndale House Publishers, Inc.

ISBN 0-8423-5564-2

Printed in the United States of America

05   04   03   02
5   4   3   2

ACCEPTANCE

What makes me acceptable to God?

Romans 3:30 *There is only one God, and there is only one way of being accepted by him. He makes people right with himself only by faith, whether they are Jews or Gentiles.*

Galatians 2:16 *We become right with God, not by doing what the law commands, but by faith in Jesus Christ. So we have believed in Christ Jesus, that we might be accepted by God because of our faith in Christ—and not because we have obeyed the law.*

Our sin separates us from a holy and perfect God. But faith in Jesus removes our sin and makes us holy and acceptable in God's sight.

How do I accept others, especially people I dislike?

Romans 14:1, 3 *Accept Christians who are weak in faith, and don't argue with them about what they think is right or wrong. . . . Those who think it is all right to eat anything must not look down on those who won't. And those who won't* eat certain foods must not condemn those who do, for God has accepted them.

Romans 15:7 *Accept each other just as Christ has accepted you; then God will be glorified.*

Judging others should be left to God. He sets the standard for accepting others.

≡**PROMISE FROM GOD:** Romans 15:7 *Accept each other just as Christ has accepted you; then God will be glorified.*

ADOPTION

Is adopting a child right for me and my family? How can I know for sure?

Matthew 18:5 *Anyone who welcomes a little child like this on my behalf is welcoming me.*

Psalm 138:8; 136:1 *The LORD will work out his plans for my life—for your faithful love, O LORD, endures forever. Give thanks to the LORD, for he is good!*

Jeremiah 1:5 *I knew you before I formed you in your mother's womb. Before you were born I set you apart and appointed you.*

There are some things in life we can't know for sure, but the Bible is clear on this: God puts a high priority on loving children. When we adopt a child and welcome him or her into our heart and life, as part of our "appointed" family, we welcome Christ.

I'm wading through all the paperwork to adopt a child. How can I deal with these months of anxious waiting?

Psalm 37:4-5 *Take delight in the LORD, and he will give you your heart's desires. Commit everything you do to the LORD. Trust him, and he will help you.*

Isaiah 60:1, 4-5 *Let your light shine for all the nations to see! . . . Look and see, for everyone is coming home! Your sons are coming from distant lands; your little daughters will be carried home. Your eyes will shine, and your hearts will thrill with joy.*

Waiting is never any fun, especially when the heart is involved. That's why it's important to keep in mind the end result: a child, over which your heart will "thrill with joy."

How can I explain my choice of adoption to others?

Psalm 127:3 *Children are a gift from the LORD; they are a reward from him.*

1 Corinthians 13:4-8 *Love is patient and kind. Love is not jealous or boastful or proud or rude. Love does not demand its own way. Love is not irritable, and it keeps no record of when it has been wronged. . . . Love never gives up, never loses faith, is always hopeful, and endures through every circumstance. Love will last forever.*

Psalm 9:1-2 *I will thank you, LORD, with all my heart; I will tell of all the marvelous things you have done. I will be filled with joy because of you. I will sing praises to your name, O Most High.*

If we choose to adopt, people may not understand that decision. And this is especially true if the child is of different ethnicity than the adoptive parents. In such situations, the best thing we can do is lovingly explain the journey we took to get to this point, that God loves all children equally, and that we feel God brought this child to our family for a particular purpose.

PROMISE FROM GOD: Psalm 138:8 *The LORD will work out his plans for my life.*

AFFIRMATION

How do we affirm one another? Why is it so important?

Romans 14:19 *Let us aim for harmony in the church and try to build each other up.*

1 Thessalonians 5:11, 13 *Encourage each other and build each other up, just as you are already doing. . . . Think highly of them and give them your wholehearted love because of their work. And remember to live peaceably with each other.*

1 Corinthians 14:26 *Well, my brothers and sisters, let's summarize what I am saying. When you meet, one will sing, another will teach, another will tell some special revelation God has given, one will speak in an unknown language, while another will interpret what is said. But everything that is done must be useful to all and build them up in the Lord.*

Hebrews 7:7 *Without question, the person who has the power to bless is always greater than the person who is blessed.*

We affirm one another through encouragement, praise, and building each other up. This gives us a great sense of worth.

How does God affirm us?

Psalm 5:12 *You bless the godly, O LORD, surrounding them with your shield of love.*

Psalm 67:1 *May God be merciful and bless us. May his face shine with favor upon us.*

1 Peter 5:10 *In his kindness God called you to his eternal glory by means of Jesus Christ. After you have suffered a little while, he will restore, support, and strengthen you, and he will place you on a firm foundation.*

2 Peter 1:2 *May God bless you with his special favor and wonderful peace as you come to know Jesus, our God and Lord, better and better.*

God affirms us through his love, his blessings, his mercy, his forgiveness, and his gift of salvation. What greater affirmation can we receive than from the Creator of the universe?

PROMISE FROM GOD: Psalm 67:1 *May God be merciful and bless us. May his face shine with favor upon us.*

ANGER

How should I deal with my own anger in relationships?

Psalm 37:8 *Stop your anger! Turn from your rage! Do not envy others—it only leads to harm.*

Proverbs 19:11 *People with good sense restrain their anger; they earn esteem by overlooking wrongs.*

Ephesians 4:26 *"Don't sin by letting anger gain control over you." Don't let the sun go down while you are still angry.*

Ephesians 4:31-32 *Get rid of all bitterness, rage, anger, harsh words, and slander, as well as all types of malicious behavior. Instead, be kind to each other, tenderhearted, forgiving one another, just as God through Christ has forgiven you.*

Anger must be dealt with quickly, before it becomes bitterness, hatred, or revenge. As hard as it sounds, kindness and forgiveness melt anger away.

When is it OK to be angry?

Numbers 25:11 *Phinehas has turned my anger away from the Israelites by displaying passionate zeal among them on my behalf.*

John 2:15-17 *[Jesus] drove out the sheep and oxen, scattered the money changers' coins and told them, "Get these things out of here. Don't turn my Father's house into a marketplace!"*

Anger at sin is not only appropriate but necessary.

PROMISE FROM GOD: Psalm 103:8 *The LORD is merciful and gracious; he is slow to get angry and full of unfailing love.*

APPROVAL

What brings God's approval?

Proverbs 12:2 *The LORD approves of those who are good, but he condemns those who plan wickedness.*

Romans 2:13 *It is not merely knowing the law that brings God's approval. Those who obey the law will be declared right in God's sight.*

Romans 3:30 *There is only one God, and there is only one way of being accepted by him. He makes people right with himself only by faith, whether they are Jews or Gentiles.*

Faith in God and obedience to his word bring approval from him.

How do I properly balance the priority of being approved by God with the desire to also be approved by others?

Proverbs 3:3-4 *Never let loyalty and kindness get away from you! Wear them like a necklace; write them deep within your heart. Then you will find favor with both God and people, and you will gain a good reputation.*

Romans 14:17-18 *The Kingdom of God is not a matter of what we eat or drink, but of living a life of goodness and peace and joy in the Holy Spirit. If you serve Christ with this attitude, you will please God. And other people will approve of you, too.*

1 Thessalonians 2:4 *We speak as messengers who have been approved by God to be entrusted with the Good News. Our purpose is to please God, not people. He is the one who examines the motives of our hearts.*

We must live to seek God's approval first. Sometimes doing what pleases God also pleases others (especially godly people), but that is not always the case. God has many enemies who love evil more than good.

Why is it important for me to show my approval of others?

Job 29:24 *When they were discouraged, I smiled at them. My look of approval was precious to them.*

Proverbs 16:15 *When the king smiles, there is life; his favor refreshes like a gentle rain.*

Your smile and words of approval may be the greatest gift someone receives today.

PROMISE FROM GOD: Numbers 6:24-26 *May the LORD bless you and protect you. May the LORD smile on you and be gracious to you. May the LORD show you his favor and give you his peace.*

BEAUTY

What does God consider beautiful?

Proverbs 19:22 *Loyalty makes a person attractive. And it is better to be poor than dishonest.*

1 Peter 3:4 *You should be known for the beauty that comes from within, the unfading beauty of a gentle and quiet spirit, which is so precious to God.*

The more we reflect God and godliness, the more we radiate his beauty. What could be more beautiful than a perfect God?

How can my words be beautiful?

Proverbs 15:26 *The LORD despises the thoughts of the wicked, but he delights in pure words.*

Proverbs 25:11 *Timely advice is as lovely as golden apples in a silver basket.*

Beautiful words are the fruit of godly thoughts and character.

How can my actions be beautiful?

1 Timothy 2:10 *Women who claim to be devoted to God should make themselves attractive by the good things they do.*

Beautiful conduct is the fruit of godly thoughts and character.

PROMISE FROM GOD: Proverbs 31:30
Charm is deceptive, and beauty does not last; but a woman who fears the LORD will be greatly praised.

BELONGING

What are the privileges of belonging to God?

Romans 8:1 *There is no condemnation for those who belong to Christ Jesus.*

Galatians 3:29 *Now that you belong to Christ, you are the true children of Abraham. You are his heirs, and now all the promises God gave to him belong to you.*

Galatians 4:7 *Now you are no longer a slave but God's own child. And since you are his child, everything he has belongs to you.*

Ephesians 1:3 *How we praise God, the Father of our Lord Jesus Christ, who has blessed us with every spiritual blessing in the heavenly realms because we belong to Christ.*

Belonging to God means you are no longer a slave to sin and therefore guilty before God. Now you can receive all the blessings he freely gives to his children. We inherit the family privileges of the Almighty.

How can I be sure I belong to God?

1 John 2:3-5 *How can we be sure that we belong to him? By obeying his commandments. If someone says, "I belong to God," but doesn't obey God's commandments, that person is a liar and does not live in the truth. But those who obey God's word really do love him. That is the way to know whether or not we live in him.*

1 John 3:10 *Now we can tell who are children of God and who are children of the Devil. Anyone who does not obey God's commands and does not love other Christians does not belong to God.*

Obeying God is a reflection of our love for him and belief in him. Since we are human, we cannot obey God perfectly all of the time. What God wants is for us to desire to always please and obey him.

PROMISE FROM GOD: Romans 8:1 *There is no condemnation for those who belong to Christ Jesus.*

How can a book written so long ago be relevant for me today?

Isaiah 40:8 *The grass withers, and the flowers fade, but the word of our God stands forever.*

2 Timothy 3:16-17 *All Scripture is inspired by God and is useful to teach us what is true and to make us realize what is wrong in our lives. It straightens us out and teaches us to do what is right. It is God's way of preparing us in every way, fully equipped for every good thing God wants us to do.*

Hebrews 4:12 *The word of God is full of living power. It is sharper than the sharpest knife, cutting deep into our innermost thoughts and desires. It exposes us for what we really are.*

Even though it was written long ago, the Bible is God's Word to us today, and it is relevant for our every need.

How can the Bible give me guidance?

Psalm 73:24 *You will keep on guiding me with your counsel, leading me to a glorious destiny.*

Psalm 119:105 *Your word is a lamp for my feet and a light for my path.*

Proverbs 6:23 *For these commands and this teaching are a lamp to light the way ahead of you.*

James 1:5 *If you need wisdom—if you want to know what God wants you to do—ask him, and he will gladly tell you.*

The Word of God is from the mind and heart of God, and who can deny that the all-wise, all-powerful, ever present God is the best guide of all?

How can the Bible give me comfort?

Psalm 119:49-50, 52, 54 *Remember your promise to me, for it is my only hope. . . . It comforts me in all my troubles. . . . I meditate on your age-old laws; O LORD, they comfort me. . . . Your principles have been the music of my life throughout the years of my pilgrimage.*

Proverbs 30:5 *Every word of God proves true. He defends all who come to him for protection.*

Romans 15:4 *Such things were written in the Scriptures long ago to teach us. They give us hope and encouragement as we wait patiently for God's promises.*

The Bible is filled with God's promises, which give us comfort and encouragement in this life as well as the confident assurance that we will one day live forever in peace and security with him.

PROMISE FROM GOD: Psalm 119:89 *Forever, O LORD, your word stands firm in heaven.*

BITTERNESS

What are some of the causes of bitter feelings?

Job 10:1 *I am disgusted with my life. Let me complain freely. I will speak in the bitterness of my soul.*

Ecclesiastes 2:17 *Now I hate life because everything done here under the sun is so irrational. Everything is meaningless, like chasing the wind.*

Proverbs 19:3 *People ruin their lives by their own foolishness and then are angry at the LORD.*

Practicing sin cultivates the fruit of sin—emptiness, bitterness, foolishness, and a sense of meaningless activity.

What is the result of unresolved bitterness?

Genesis 27:42 *[Rebekah] sent for Jacob and told him, "Esau is threatening to kill you."*

Job 5:2 *Surely resentment destroys the fool, and jealousy kills the simple.*

Proverbs 27:3 *A stone is heavy and sand is weighty, but the resentment caused by a fool is heavier than both.*

Unresolved bitterness leads to hatred, anger, jealousy, and revenge. It keeps us from fellowship with God and others and blinds us to God's blessings.

How do I deal with bitterness toward others?

Mark 11:25 *When you are praying, first forgive anyone you are holding a grudge against, so that your Father in heaven will forgive your sins, too.*

Acts 8:22-23 *Turn from your wickedness and pray to the Lord. Perhaps he will forgive your evil thoughts, for I can see that you are full of bitterness and held captive by sin.*

Ephesians 4:31-32 *Get rid of all bitterness, rage, anger, harsh words, and slander, as well as all types of malicious behavior. Instead, be kind to each other, tenderhearted, forgiving one another, just as God through Christ has forgiven you.*

Forgiveness lifts burdens, cancels debts, and frees us from chains of bitterness.

PROMISE FROM GOD: Titus 1:15 *Everything is pure to those whose hearts are pure.*

BLESSINGS
AND THANKS

What are the qualities in my life that bring God's blessings?

Psalm 128:1 *How happy are those who fear the LORD— all who follow his ways!*

Psalm 146:5 *Happy are those who have the God of Israel as their helper, whose hope is in the LORD their God.*

Jeremiah 17:7 *Blessed are those who trust in the LORD and have made the LORD their hope and confidence.*

A life focused on God brings joy to God and many blessings to you.

What kinds of blessings does God send to my family?

Numbers 6:24-26 *May the LORD bless you and protect you. May the LORD smile on you and be gracious to you. May the LORD show you his favor and give you his peace.*

Success and prosperity are not the most common blessings from God, but rather peace, comfort, joy, fellowship with God, hope, and eternal life with him.

How can I be a blessing to my family?

Romans 1:11-12 *I long to visit you so I can share a spiritual blessing with you that will help you grow strong in the Lord. I'm eager to encourage you in your faith, but I also want to be encouraged by yours. In this way, each of us will be a blessing to the other.*

2 Corinthians 2:14 *Thanks be to God, who made us his captives and leads us along in Christ's triumphal procession. Now wherever we go he uses us to tell others about the Lord and to spread the Good News like a sweet perfume.*

As we share the blessings God has poured on us, we bless others as well. Encouraging others with God's Good News is one of the most rewarding of his blessings.

Why is it important to raise thankful children?

Psalm 50:23 *Giving thanks is a sacrifice that truly honors me. If you keep to my path, I will reveal to you the salvation of God.*

Psalm 92:1 *It is good to give thanks to the LORD, to sing praises to the Most High.*

Luke 17:16 *He fell face down on the ground at Jesus' feet, thanking him for what he had done.*

When we give thanks to God, we honor him and praise him. Also, we honor others when we give thanks to them, respecting them for who they are and what they have done.

How do I develop an attitude of thanksgiving in myself and my family?

Psalm 9:1 *I will thank you, LORD, with all my heart; I will tell of all the marvelous things you have done.*

Psalm 92:2 *It is good to proclaim your unfailing love in the morning, your faithfulness in the evening.*

Philippians 1:3 *Every time I think of you, I give thanks to my God.*

Colossians 3:15 *Let the peace that comes from Christ rule in your hearts. For as members of one body you are all called to live in peace. And always be thankful.*

1 Timothy 4:4 *Since everything God created is good, we should not reject any of it. We may receive it gladly, with thankful hearts.*

Cultivate thankfulness by giving thanks regularly as a family. Set aside time every day to talk about things you are thankful for.

How can I teach my children to express thankfulness?

Psalm 111:1-2 *Praise the LORD! I will thank the LORD with all my heart as I meet with his godly people. How amazing are the deeds of the LORD! All who delight in him should ponder them.*

Psalm 116:17 *I will offer you a sacrifice of thanksgiving and call on the name of the LORD.*

Psalm 119:7 *When I learn your righteous laws, I will thank you by living as I should!*

Psalm 147:7 *Sing out your thanks to the LORD; sing praises to our God, accompanied by harps.*

Colossians 2:7 *Let your roots grow down into him and draw up nourishment from him, so you will grow in faith, strong and vigorous in the truth you were taught. Let your lives overflow with thanksgiving for all he has done.*

Colossians 4:2 *Devote yourselves to prayer with an alert mind and a thankful heart.*

We can help our children show thankfulness to God through prayer, through a grateful heart, through singing and praise, by living as we should, and through service.

Regardless of circumstances, what can I always be thankful for?

1 Chronicles 16:34 *Give thanks to the LORD, for he is good! His faithful love endures forever.*

Psalm 7:17 *I will thank the LORD because he is just; I will sing praise to the name of the LORD Most High.*

Psalm 138:2 *I bow before your holy Temple as I worship. I will give thanks to your name for your unfailing love and faithfulness, because your promises are backed by all the honor of your name.*

1 Corinthians 15:57 *How we thank God, who gives us victory over sin and death through Jesus Christ our Lord!*

2 Corinthians 9:15 *Thank God for his Son—a gift too wonderful for words!*

Ephesians 2:8 *God saved you by his special favor when you believed.*

1 Thessalonians 5:18 *No matter what happens, always be thankful, for this is God's will for you who belong to Christ Jesus.*

1 Timothy 1:12 *How thankful I am to Christ Jesus our Lord for considering me trustworthy and appointing me to serve him.*

We can thank the Lord for being good and just, and we

can thank him for who he is. We can thank him also for his love for us; for his faithfulness; for sending his Son, Jesus; and for his mercy. We can thank him for victory over death and for keeping his promises.

PROMISE FROM GOD: 1 Chronicles 16:34
Give thanks to the LORD, for he is good! His faithful love endures forever.

BOREDOM

Why do I get bored?

Hebrews 6:11-12 *Our great desire is that you will keep right on loving others as long as life lasts, in order to make certain that what you hope for will come true. Then you will not become spiritually dull and indifferent.*

We get bored when we lose hope. It is hope that enables us to press on even when life gets difficult.

What are signs of boredom?

Proverbs 26:14 *As a door turns back and forth on its hinges, so the lazy person turns over in bed.*

Ecclesiastes 2:23 *Their days of labor are filled with pain and grief; even at night they cannot rest. It is all utterly meaningless.*

Galatians 6:9 *Don't get tired of doing what is good. Don't get discouraged and give up, for we will reap a harvest of blessing at the appropriate time.*

Getting tired of what is good, a sense of meaninglessness, laziness—these are all signs of boredom.

How can the Christian life eliminate boredom?

Nehemiah 8:10   *The joy of the LORD is your strength!*

Ephesians 5:1-2   *Follow God's example in everything you do. . . . Live a life filled with love for others, following the example of Christ.*

If you really try to follow Christ's example every day, you will never become bored!

PROMISE FROM GOD: Philippians 2:4 *Don't think only about your own affairs, but be interested in others, too, and what they are doing.*

*B*OUNDARIES

What are the benefits of boundaries?

Psalm 36:1 *Sin whispers to the wicked, deep within their hearts. They have no fear of God to restrain them.*

Boundaries of love from a loving God protect us from the evil one.

What are God's boundaries for me?

Micah 6:8 *No, O people, the LORD has already told you what is good, and this is what he requires: to do what is right, to love mercy, and to walk humbly with your God.*

God's boundaries are his loving restraints to keep us from falling away from him.

How do I set boundaries for myself?

1 Corinthians 10:29-33 *It might not be a matter of conscience for you, but it is for the other person. . . . I try to please everyone in everything I do. I don't just do what I like or what is best for me, but what is best for them so they may be saved.*

God's Word clearly states certain rules that we must live by. But God's Word also talks much about following the spirit of his law, doing things that will not cause another to stumble, even though those things might technically be appropriate.

PROMISE FROM GOD: Exodus 34:24 *I will enlarge your boundaries.*

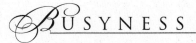

$\mathcal{B}$USYNESS

What are the benefits of being busy?

Proverbs 31:17, 27 *She is energetic and strong, a hard worker. . . . She carefully watches all that goes on in her household and does not have to bear the consequences of laziness.*

Ecclesiastes 11:6 *Be sure to stay busy and plant a variety of crops, for you never know which will grow—perhaps they all will.*

Rich harvests cannot come from lazy fingers. If we want fruitfulness in any facet of our life, we must get busy now.

What are the dangers of busyness?

Psalm 39:6 *We are merely moving shadows, and all our busy rushing ends in nothing. We heap up wealth for someone else to spend.*

Proverbs 19:2 *Zeal without knowledge is not good; a person who moves too quickly may go the wrong way.*

Haggai 1:9 *You hoped for rich harvests, but they were poor. And when you brought your harvest home, I blew it away. Why? Because my house lies in ruins, says the LORD Almighty, while you are all busy building your own fine houses.*

Never confuse activity with accomplishment. Activity without God can come up empty-handed.

How can I find rest from the busyness of life?

Exodus 34:21 *Six days are set aside for work, but on the Sabbath day you must rest, even during the seasons of plowing and harvest.*

Psalm 23:2 *He lets me rest in green meadows; he leads me beside peaceful streams.*

Psalm 91:1 *Those who live in the shelter of the Most High will find rest in the shadow of the Almighty.*

Psalm 145:5 *I will meditate on your majestic, glorious splendor and your wonderful miracles.*

God is both the model and the source of rest. As God rested after creation was finished, so he provides and encourages rest from our labors.

PROMISE FROM GOD: Matthew 11:28-29 *Then Jesus said, "Come to me, all of you who are weary and* *carry heavy burdens, and I will give you rest. Take my yoke upon you. Let me teach you, because I am humble and gentle, and you will find rest for your souls.*

CAREER

See WORK

CARING

How does God show his care for me?

Psalm 78:72 *He cared for them with a true heart and led them with skillful hands.*

Psalm 121:7-8 *The LORD keeps you from all evil and preserves your life. The LORD keeps watch over you as you come and go, both now and forever.*

Psalm 145:18-20 *The LORD is close to all who call on him, yes, to all who call on him sincerely. He fulfills the desires of those who fear him; he hears their cries for help and rescues them. The LORD protects all those who love him, but he destroys the wicked.*

Matthew 6:30 *If God cares so wonderfully for flowers that are here today and gone tomorrow, won't he more surely care for you? You have so little faith!*

1 Peter 5:7 *Give all your worries and cares to God, for he cares about what happens to you.*

God protects, provides, and preserves us—now and forever.

How can I show others I care?

Matthew 25:36 *I was naked, and you gave me clothing. I was sick, and you cared for me. I was in prison, and you visited me.*

Luke 10:34-35 *Kneeling beside him, the Samaritan soothed his wounds with medicine and bandaged them. Then he put the man on his own donkey and took him to an inn, where he took care of him. The next day he handed the innkeeper two pieces of silver and told him to take care of the man. "If his bill runs higher than that," he said, "I'll pay the difference the next time I am here."*

1 Corinthians 12:25 *This makes for harmony among the members, so that all the members care for each other equally.*

As God shows his care for us by protecting, providing, and preserving, so we can show his care to others by doing the same for them.

PROMISE FROM GOD: 1 Peter 5:7 *Give all your worries and cares to God, for he cares about what happens to you.*

CELEBRATION

What causes God to celebrate?

Ezekiel 35:15 *You rejoiced at the desolation of Israel's inheritance. Now I will rejoice at yours! You will be wiped out, you people of Mount Seir and all who live in Edom! Then you will know that I am the LORD!*

Matthew 25:23 *The master said, "Well done, my good and faithful servant. You have been faithful in handling this small amount, so now I will give you many more responsibilities. Let's celebrate together!"*

Luke 15:10 *In the same way, there is joy in the presence of God's angels when even one sinner repents.*
God celebrates the defeat of sin and evil, the salvation of the lost, and the daily joys and successes of his people.

What is the importance of family in celebration?

Exodus 12:26 *Then your children will ask, "What does all this mean? What is this ceremony about?"*

Nehemiah 12:43 *Many sacrifices were offered on that joyous day, for God had given the people cause for great joy. The women and children also participated in the celebration, and the joy of the people of Jerusalem could be heard far away.*

Esther 9:28 *These days would be remembered and kept from generation to generation and celebrated by every family throughout the provinces and cities of the empire.*
As we celebrate the Lord with our family, we role model the Lord's presence in our lives. This is the greatest inheritance we can give to our children and grandchildren; it is a treasure to be passed on to future generations.

Regardless of my personal circumstances, what can I always celebrate?

Psalm 135:3 *Praise the LORD, for the LORD is good; celebrate his wonderful name with music.*

Isaiah 49:13 *Sing for joy, O heavens! Rejoice, O earth! Burst into song, O mountains! For the LORD has comforted his people and will have compassion on them in their sorrow.*

Sometimes we can celebrate the joy of good circumstances, but always we can celebrate the Lord himself!

PROMISE FROM GOD: Psalm 5:11 *Let all who take refuge in you rejoice; let them sing joyful praises forever. Protect them, so all who love your name may be filled with joy.*

CHANGE

How do I change the areas in my life that need to be changed?

Acts 3:19 *Turn from your sins and turn to God, so you can be cleansed of your sins.*

If you haven't repented of your sins, this is the greatest change in your life you need to make.

Psalm 51:10 *Create in me a clean heart, O God. Renew a right spirit within me.*

Romans 12:2 *Don't copy the behavior and customs of this world, but let God transform you into a new person by changing the way you think. Then you will know what God wants you to do, and you will know how good and pleasing and perfect his will really is.*

Ephesians 4:23-24 *Instead, there must be a spiritual renewal of your thoughts and attitudes. You must display a new nature because you are a new person, created in God's likeness—righteous, holy, and true.*

Real and dynamic change occurs when we ask God for

a new heart filled with Christ's love, a new spirit to show us how to live, a new way of thinking, and a new attitude.

Colossians 3:10 *In its place you have clothed yourselves with a brand-new nature that is continually being renewed as you learn more and more about Christ, who created this new nature within you.*

Be patient with yourself, as change is often a process.

Does God ever change?

Lamentations 5:19 *LORD, you remain the same forever! Your throne continues from generation to generation.*

Malachi 3:6 *I am the LORD, and I do not change.*

Hebrews 13:8 *Jesus Christ is the same yesterday, today, and forever.*

James 1:17 *Whatever is good and perfect comes to us from God above, who created all heaven's lights. Unlike them, he never changes or casts shifting shadows.*

Not only does God live forever, but he remains unchanged forever. He is a God of eternal consistency.

PROMISE FROM GOD: Isaiah 40:8 *The grass withers, and the flowers fade, but the word of our God stands forever.*

CHARACTER

Why is building character so hard?

Romans 5:4 *Endurance develops strength of character in us, and character strengthens our confident expectation of salvation.*

James 1:2-4 *Dear brothers and sisters, whenever trouble comes your way, let it be an opportunity for joy. For when your faith is tested, your endurance has a chance to grow. So let it grow, for when your endurance is fully developed, you will be strong in character and ready for anything.*

Developing character is a process that comes only through time and testing. It is trial and error. Pain, trials, and temptation refine us so that over time we will be better equipped and more experienced to deal with them.

PROMISE FROM GOD: Matthew 5:8 *God blesses those whose hearts are pure, for they will see God.*

CHILDREN

What childlike characteristics should an adult retain?

Matthew 18:3-4 *Then he said, "I assure you, unless you turn from your sins and become as little children, you will never get into the Kingdom of Heaven. Therefore, anyone who becomes as humble as this little child is the greatest in the Kingdom of Heaven."*

Mark 10:14-15 *But when Jesus saw what was happening he said to them, "Let the children come to me. Don't stop them! For the Kingdom of God belongs to such as these. I assure you, anyone who doesn't have their kind of faith will never get into the Kingdom of God."*

Luke 10:21 *Then Jesus was filled with the joy of the Holy Spirit and said, "O Father, Lord of heaven and earth, thank you for hiding the truth from those who think themselves*

*so wise and clever, and for revealing it to the childlike. Yes,
Father, it pleased you to do it this way."*

Like children, we must cultivate simple faith and humility
before the Lord.

What relationship did God intend between parents and their children?

Ephesians 6:1-4 *Children, obey your parents because
you belong to the Lord, for this is the right thing to do.
"Honor your father and mother." This is the first of the Ten
Commandments that ends with a promise. And this is the
promise: If you honor your father and mother, "you will live
a long life, full of blessing." And now a word to you fathers.
Don't make your children angry by the way you treat them.
Rather, bring them up with the discipline and instruction
approved by the Lord.*

Parents are entrusted with the responsibility of teaching
their children to walk in God's ways and of disciplining
them in love. Children are to respond with respect and
obedience.

How can I most effectively teach my child about God and his ways?

Exodus 10:2 *You will be able to tell wonderful stories to
your children and grandchildren about the marvelous things
I am doing among the Egyptians to prove that I am the LORD.*

Deuteronomy 11:18-19 *So commit yourselves completely
to these words of mine. Tie them to your hands as a reminder,
and wear them on your forehead. Teach them to your children.
Talk about them when you are at home and when you are
away on a journey, when you are lying down and when you
are getting up again.*

Proverbs 22:6 *Teach your children to choose the right path, and when they are older, they will remain upon it.*

As parents, we have the remarkable privilege of living what we want our children to learn (role modeling), sharing God's truth we want them to hear (precepts), guiding them in which way to go (choices), and then watching with joy as our work continues to future generations.

How are children to relate to parents?

Exodus 20:12 *Honor your father and mother. Then you will live a long, full life in the land the LORD your God will give you.*

Ephesians 6:1 *Children, obey your parents because you belong to the Lord.*

Children have a responsibility to honor and show respect to their parents.

PROMISE FROM GOD: Isaiah 59:21 *My Spirit will not leave them, and neither will these words I have given you. They will be on your lips and on the lips of your children and your children's children forever.*

CHRISTLIKENESS

What is meant by "Christlikeness"?

Luke 9:23 *Then he said to the crowd, "If any of you wants to be my follower, you must put aside your selfish ambition, shoulder your cross daily, and follow me."*

Christlikeness involves selflessly following Christ.

Luke 6:36 *You must be compassionate, just as your Father is compassionate.*

A compassionate lifestyle is a sign of Christlikeness.

1 Peter 2:21-23 *Christ, who suffered for you, is your example. Follow in his steps. . . . He did not retaliate when he was insulted. When he suffered, he did not threaten to get even. He left his case in the hands of God, who always judges fairly.*

Christlikeness is following in Christ's footsteps. As we follow our Lord, we attract others to follow him also.

John 13:14-15 *Since I, the Lord and Teacher, have washed your feet, you ought to wash each other's feet. I have given you an example to follow. Do as I have done to you.*

A life of humble service is a necessary part of Christ-likeness.

How do I become like Christ?

2 Corinthians 3:18 *All of us have had that veil removed so that we can be mirrors that brightly reflect the glory of the Lord. And as the Spirit of the Lord works within us, we become more and more like him and reflect his glory even more.*

Ephesians 4:15 *We will hold to the truth in love, becoming more and more in every way like Christ, who is the head of his body, the church.*

Philippians 1:6 *I am sure that God, who began the good work within you, will continue his work until it is finally finished on that day when Christ Jesus comes back again.*

We become more like Christ by carefully studying how he lived and loved. Then we invite him to work his powerful love through us.

How can my Christlike character affect my home?

1 Corinthians 7:14 *The Christian wife brings holiness to her marriage, and the Christian husband brings holiness to his marriage. Otherwise, your children would not have a godly influence, but now they are set apart for him.*

1 Peter 3:1-2 *In the same way, you wives must accept the authority of your husbands, even those who refuse to accept the Good News. Your godly lives will speak to them better than any words. They will be won over by watching your pure, godly behavior.*

How you model your faith in Christ will have an incredible influence upon your children, as well as upon future generations.

PROMISE FROM GOD: Galatians 2:20 *I myself no longer live, but Christ lives in me. So I live my life in this earthly body by trusting in the Son of God, who loved me and gave himself for me.*

CHURCH AND COMMUNITY

Why is it important that my family attend church?

Acts 2:47 *Each day the Lord added to their group those who were being saved.*

The church is a gathering place for all who are saved by faith in Christ.

1 Corinthians 3:16-17 *Don't you realize that all of you together are the temple of God and that the Spirit of God lives in you? God will bring ruin upon anyone who ruins this temple. For God's temple is holy, and you Christians are that temple.*

By spending time in the church, we can learn more about God's holiness.

1 Corinthians 12:12-13 *The human body has many parts, but the many parts make up only one body. So it is with the body of Christ. Some of us are Jews, some are Gentiles, some are slaves, and some are free. But we have all been baptized into Christ's body by one Spirit, and we have all received the same Spirit.*

The church is a place where Christians learn to work together in unity. It also teaches us about the reconciliation between different people that is possible in Christ by his Spirit.

Ephesians 4:11-12 *He is the one who gave these gifts to the church: the apostles, the prophets, the evangelists, and the pastors and teachers. Their responsibility is to equip God's people to do his work and build up the church, the body of Christ.*

The church exists in part to equip God's people to do God's work and to encourage them in their faith.

Revelation 19:7-8 *Let us be glad and rejoice and honor him. For the time has come for the wedding feast of the Lamb, and his bride has prepared herself. She is permitted to wear the finest white linen.*

The church is Christ's bride—a picture of the intimate fellowship that God's people will enjoy with him.

Why is it important that we meet together as a community of believers?

Matthew 18:20 *Where two or three gather together because they are mine, I am there among them.*

Because Jesus promises to be there with us.

Psalm 55:14 *What good fellowship we enjoyed as we walked together to the house of God.*

Because we will enjoy the fellowship of other believers.

1 Corinthians 11:33 *So, dear brothers and sisters, when you gather for the Lord's Supper, wait for each other.*

1 Corinthians 10:16-17 *When we bless the cup at the Lord's Table, aren't we sharing in the benefits of the blood of Christ? And when we break the loaf of bread, aren't we sharing in the benefits of the body of Christ? And we all eat from one loaf, showing that we are one body.*

Because we can celebrate the Lord together.

Acts 4:24 *Then all the believers were united as they lifted their voices in prayer: "O Sovereign Lord, Creator of heaven and earth, the sea, and everything in them . . ."*

Acts 12:12 *He went to the home of Mary, the mother of John Mark, where many were gathered for prayer.*

Because we can pray together.

How can my family benefit the community?

Romans 12:5-6 *We are all parts of his one body, and each of us has different work to do. And since we are all one body in Christ, we belong to each other, and each of us needs all the others. God has given each of us the ability to do certain things well.*

1 Corinthians 14:12 *Since you are so eager to have spiritual gifts, ask God for those that will be of real help to the whole church.*

Since God has given each person unique personal gifts, we should find the best way to invest those gifts for him.

PROMISE FROM GOD: Matthew 18:20 *Where two or three gather together because they are mine, I am there among them.*

COMFORT

How does God comfort me in my times of distress?

Romans 8:26 *The Holy Spirit helps us in our distress. For we don't even know what we should pray for, nor how we should pray. But the Holy Spirit prays for us with groanings that cannot be expressed in words.*

He prays for me.

Psalm 10:17 *LORD, you know the hopes of the helpless. Surely you will listen to their cries and comfort them.*

He listens to me.

Psalm 94:19 *When doubts filled my mind, your comfort gave me renewed hope and cheer.*

He gives me hope and cheer.

Psalm 119:50-52 *Your promise revives me; it comforts me in all my troubles. . . . I meditate on your age-old laws; O LORD, they comfort me.*

He revives me with his word.

Psalm 119:76 *Now let your unfailing love comfort me, just as you promised me, your servant.*
He loves me.

2 Thessalonians 2:16-17 *May our Lord Jesus Christ and God our Father, who loved us and in his special favor gave us everlasting comfort and good hope, comfort your hearts and give you strength in every good thing you do and say.*
He gives us eternal hope.

How can I comfort others?

Job 42:11 *Then all his brothers, sisters, and former friends came and feasted with him in his home. And they consoled him and comforted him because of all the trials the LORD had brought against him. And each of them brought him a gift of money and a gold ring.*
By my presence.

Job 21:2 *Listen closely to what I am saying. You can console me by listening to me.*
By listening.

Ruth 2:13 *"I hope I continue to please you, sir," she replied. "You have comforted me by speaking so kindly to me, even though I am not as worthy as your workers."*

1 Corinthians 14:3 *But one who prophesies is helping others grow in the Lord, encouraging and comforting them.*
By my words.

Philemon 1:7 *I myself have gained much joy and comfort from your love, my brother, because your kindness has so often refreshed the hearts of God's people.*
By my love expressed through kindness.

PROMISE FROM GOD: 2 Thessalonians 2:16-17 *May our Lord Jesus Christ who gave us everlasting comfort and good hope, comfort your hearts and give you strength in every good thing you do and say.*

COMMUNITY

See CHURCH AND COMMUNITY

COMPASSION

How does God show his compassion to me?

Psalm 103:8 *The LORD is merciful and gracious; he is slow to get angry and full of unfailing love.*

Psalm 103:13 *The LORD is like a father to his children, tender and compassionate to those who fear him.*

God shows his compassion to us by giving us blessings we don't deserve and by not giving us what we deserve. Instead he forgives us and restores us to what we were intended to be.

How can I show compassion to others?

2 Corinthians 8:9 *You know how full of love and kindness our Lord Jesus Christ was. Though he was very rich, yet for your sakes he became poor, so that by his poverty he could make you rich.*

Christ in his love for us gave up his most high position to come to earth and die for us. Our response should be to throw out our pride and show compassion to those around us, even when it takes us out of our comfort zone.

PROMISE FROM GOD: Psalm 72:12 *He will rescue the poor when they cry to him; he will help the oppressed, who have no one to defend them.*

COMPLAINING

What are the dangers of complaining?

James 4:11 *Don't speak evil against each other, my dear brothers and sisters. If you criticize each other and condemn each other, then you are criticizing and condemning God's law. But you are not a judge who can decide whether the law is right or wrong. Your job is to obey it.*

James 5:9 *Don't grumble about each other, my brothers and sisters, or God will judge you. For look! The great Judge is coming. He is standing at the door!*

Complaining about others is indirectly complaining about God and his Word.

What should I do instead of complaining?

Philippians 2:14-15 *In everything you do, stay away from complaining and arguing, so that no one can speak a word of blame against you.*

Instead of complaining about others, be a role model to them. Role modeling at its best lifts others up, while complaining puts them down.

Lamentations 3:39-40 *Then why should we, mere humans, complain when we are punished for our sins? Instead, let us test and examine our ways. Let us turn again in repentance to the LORD.*

Instead of complaining about the sins of others, let's repent of our own sins.

Luke 6:37 *Stop judging others, and you will not be judged. Stop criticizing others, or it will all come back on you. If you forgive others, you will be forgiven.*

Instead of complaining about the weaknesses of others, let's forgive them as we would like to be forgiven.

What effect does my complaining have on others?

Proverbs 19:13 *A foolish child is a calamity to a father; a nagging wife annoys like a constant dripping.*

Proverbs 21:19 *It is better to live alone in the desert than with a crabby, complaining wife.*

No one likes to be around a constant complainer.

PROMISE FROM GOD: Ephesians 4:29 *Let everything you say be good and helpful, so that your words will be an encouragement to those who hear them.*

COMPROMISE

When is compromise inappropriate?

Romans 6:12 *Do not let sin control the way you live; do not give in to its lustful desires.*

When the compromise involves sin of any kind

1 Samuel 15:24 *Then Saul finally admitted, "Yes, I have sinned. I have disobeyed your instructions and the LORD's command, for I was afraid of the people and did what they demanded."*

Exodus 23:2 *Do not join a crowd that intends to do evil.*

3 John 1:11 *Dear friend, don't let this bad example influence you. Follow only what is good.*

When the compromise is motivated by people-pleasing or following the bad example of others

How do I respond appropriately when I am tempted to compromise God's ways?

1 Chronicles 22:13 *For if you carefully obey the laws and regulations that the LORD gave to Israel through Moses, you will be successful. Be strong and courageous; do not be afraid or lose heart!*

1 Corinthians 10:13 *But remember that the temptations that come into your life are no different from what others experience. And God is faithful. He will keep the temptation from becoming so strong that you can't stand up against it. When you are tempted, he will show you a way out so that you will not give in to it.*

Ephesians 6:11 *Put on all of God's armor so that you will be able to stand firm against all strategies and tricks of the Devil.*

It is never appropriate to compromise your Christian convictions.

PROMISE FROM GOD: 1 Chronicles 22:13
*For if you carefully obey the laws and regulations that the
LORD gave to Israel through Moses, you will be successful.
Be strong and courageous; do not be afraid or lose heart!*

CONFESSION

What is my responsibility regarding my confession of Christ?

Romans 10:9 *If you confess with your mouth that Jesus
is Lord and believe in your heart that God raised him from
the dead, you will be saved.*

Matthew 10:32 *If anyone acknowledges me publicly here
on earth, I will openly acknowledge that person before my
Father in heaven.*

1 John 2:4 *If someone says, "I belong to God," but doesn't
obey God's commandments, that person is a liar and does not
live in the truth.*

If we want Christ to acknowledge us as his redeemed,
we must acknowledge him as our Redeemer. He will
claim us in the Day of Judgment as we claim him now.

What is involved in true confession?

Psalm 38:18 *But I confess my sins; I am deeply sorry
for what I have done.*

Psalm 51:3-6, 17 *For I recognize my shameful deeds—
they haunt me day and night. Against you, and you alone, have
I sinned; I have done what is evil in your sight. . . . But you
desire honesty from the heart, so you can teach me to be wise*

*in my inmost being. The sacrifice you want is a broken spirit.
A broken and repentant heart, O God, you will not despise.*

Sorrow for our sin, humility before God, seeking God
and his forgiveness, turning to God in prayer, turning
from sin—these are ingredients of confession to God.

Does God's forgiveness always follow true confession?

Psalm 65:3 *Though our hearts are filled with sins, you
forgive them all.*

Psalm 86:5 *O Lord, you are so good, so ready to forgive,
so full of unfailing love for all who ask your aid.*

1 John 1:9 *If we confess our sins to him, he is faithful
and just to forgive us and to cleanse us from every wrong.*

God's supply of forgiveness far exceeds the number of
times we could ever go to him for forgiveness.

**In addition to forgiveness, what results from
confession?**

Psalm 32:5 *Finally, I confessed all my sins to you and
stopped trying to hide them. I said to myself, "I will confess
my rebellion to the LORD." And you forgave me! All my guilt
is gone.*

God removes our guilt.

Psalm 51:12 *Restore to me again the joy of your salvation,
and make me willing to obey you.*

God restores our joy and willing obedience.

James 5:16 *Confess your sins to each other and pray for
each other so that you may be healed. The earnest prayer
of a righteous person has great power and wonderful results.*

God heals us.

PROMISE FROM GOD: 1 John 1:9 *If we confess our sins to him, he is faithful and just to forgive us and to cleanse us from every wrong.*

CONFLICT AND CONFRONTATION

What causes conflict in the home?

Proverbs 13:10 *Pride leads to arguments.*

Proverbs 28:25 *Greed causes fighting.*

Proverbs 30:33 *Anger causes quarrels.*

James 4:1 *What is causing the quarrels and fights among you? Isn't it the whole army of evil desires at war within you?*

Pride, greed, anger—these are all aspects of our sinful human nature, and these are the things that bring us into conflict with others, especially in our own families.

How do I keep conflict among my children to a minimum?

Proverbs 26:17 *Yanking a dog's ears is as foolish as interfering in someone else's argument.*

It is sometimes tempting to step into an argument in process in order to "solve it," but doing so often only heats up the issue.

Romans 12:18 *Do your part to live in peace with everyone, as much as possible.*

CONFLICT AND
CONFRONTATION

Matthew 5:9 *God blesses those who work for peace,*
for they will be called the children of God.
As Christ's ambassadors, we need to work actively to be
at peace with others.

Ephesians 4:3 *Always keep yourselves united in the Holy*
Spirit, and bind yourselves together with peace.
Spiritual unity and fellowship with God through the Holy
Spirit will often help us to bring unity and peace to our
family relationships.

Why is it important that I confront my children when they've done something wrong?

Ephesians 5:11 *Take no part in the worthless deeds*
of evil and darkness; instead, rebuke and expose them.
Evil and wickedness must be confronted, or they may
consume us.

2 Samuel 12:1, 7 *So the LORD sent Nathan the prophet*
to tell David this story: . . . Then Nathan said to David,
"You are that man!"

Luke 17:3 *If another believer sins, rebuke him; then if he*
repents, forgive him.
Confronting someone who does wrong may lead that
person back into reconciliation with God and others.

What is the best way to effectively confront my children when they've done something wrong?

Proverbs 27:5 *An open rebuke is better than hidden love!*

2 Timothy 2:24-25 *The Lord's servants must not*
quarrel but must be kind to everyone. They must be able to
teach effectively and be patient with difficult people. They

should gently teach those who oppose the truth. Perhaps God will change those people's hearts, and they will believe the truth.

Confront openly but without quarreling and with kindness. Teach effectively and gently, with patience. Then let God change your child's heart!

2 Timothy 1:7 *For God has not given us a spirit of fear and timidity, but of power, love, and self-discipline.*

Confront in power, love, and self-discipline!

How can I help my children respond to conflict and confrontation?

Proverbs 24:26 *It is an honor to receive an honest reply.*

Receive confrontation as an honor if it causes you to repent. You should be honored that someone cares enough about you to want what is best for you.

Proverbs 19:25 *If you punish a mocker, the simple-minded will learn a lesson; if you reprove the wise, they will be all the wiser.*

Confrontation should increase our wisdom.

≡PROMISE FROM GOD: 2 Timothy 2:25 *Gently teach those who oppose the truth. Perhaps God will change those people's hearts, and they will believe the truth.*

CONFRONTATION

See CONFLICT AND CONFRONTATION

CONSISTENCY

How can I possibly obey all God's commandments consistently? As a mom, I find myself failing at most of them at one time or another.

Deuteronomy 8:1 *Be careful to obey all the commands I am giving you today.*

1 John 2:3 *How can we be sure that we belong to him? By obeying his commandments.*

The rule for perfect living is to obey all of God's commandments. But even moms aren't perfect. The key, therefore, is to consistently try to obey God's commandments, realizing that we will fail at some. At the point of our failure we need to consistently seek Jesus and his forgiveness.

How important is consistency to my role as a parent?

Titus 2:7 *Let everything you do reflect the integrity and seriousness of your teaching.*

Consistency is especially important in parenting. Children may not accept your words or beliefs, but if your lifestyle is admirable, more often than not they are compelled to trust and admire you.

I know it's important that my children see me living a consistent life, but where can I find a role model for consistency?

Hebrews 13:8-9 *Jesus Christ is the same yesterday, today, and forever. So do not be attracted by strange, new ideas.*

Jesus is the role model for consistency in belief, character, and life.

So what does consistent living look like?

James 3:13 *If you are wise and understand God's ways, live a life of steady goodness so that only good deeds will pour forth.*

When we live a consistent life, our children can anticipate our actions tomorrow by our actions today and yesterday.

PROMISE FROM GOD: Malachi 3:6 *I am the LORD, and I do not change.*

CONTENTMENT

How can I find contentment regardless of life's circumstances?

2 Corinthians 12:10 *Since I know it is all for Christ's good, I am quite content with my weaknesses and with insults, hardships, persecutions, and calamities. For when I am weak, then I am strong.*

Philippians 4:11-13 *I have learned how to get along happily whether I have much or little. I know how to live on almost nothing or with everything. I have learned the secret of living in every situation, whether it is with a full stomach or empty, with plenty or little. For I can do everything with the help of Christ who gives me the strength I need.*

2 Peter 1:3 *As we know Jesus better, his divine power gives us everything we need for living a godly life. He has called us to receive his own glory and goodness!*

CONTENTMENT

When we depend on circumstances for our contentment, we become unhappy when things don't go our way. When we depend on Jesus for our contentment, we are secure because he never fails.

In what or whom should I find contentment?

Psalm 90:14 *Satisfy us in the morning with your unfailing love, so we may sing for joy to the end of our lives.*

Psalm 107:8-9 *Let them praise the LORD for his great love and for all his wonderful deeds to them. For he satisfies the thirsty and fills the hungry with good things.*

Psalm 119:35 *Make me walk along the path of your commands, for that is where my happiness is found.*

God, who *is* perfect peace, can certainly give *us* perfect peace.

How can I be a source of contentment in my relationships?

Psalm 106:3 *Happy are those who deal justly with others and always do what is right.*

Psalm 119:1 *Happy are people of integrity, who follow the law of the LORD.*

Psalm 133:1 *How wonderful it is, how pleasant, when brothers live together in harmony!*

As God is the ultimate source of contentment to us, so our godly conduct toward others can be a source of God's contentment through us.

PROMISE FROM GOD: Psalm 107:9 *He satisfies the thirsty and fills the hungry with good things.*

$\mathcal{C}$ONTROL

With all that is out of control in the world, how can I assure my children that God is still in control?

Acts 17:31 *He has set a day for judging the world with justice.*

Even though we may not understand the sin and evil in the world, we can trust the Lord of heaven and earth to one day work out his great redemptive purpose.

Colossians 1:17 *He existed before everything else began, and he holds all creation together.*

Jesus Christ is Lord even of all unseen spiritual forces and can be trusted with the ultimate control of the universe.

Ephesians 1:22 *And God has put all things under the authority of Christ, and he gave him this authority for the benefit of the church.*

By the same power that raised him from the dead, Jesus will one day bring all things under his sovereign control.

Hebrews 1:10 *Lord, in the beginning you laid the foundation of the earth, and the heavens are the work of your hands.*

Even though our human perspective is limited, Jesus Christ is the supreme ruler of all things.

How can I learn to have more self-control, especially with my children?

CONTROL

2 Peter 1:5-8 *Make every effort to apply the benefits of these promises to your life. . . . Knowing God leads to self-control. Self-control leads to patient endurance, and patient endurance leads to godliness. Godliness leads to love for other Christians, and finally you will grow to have genuine love for everyone.*

As we intentionally spend time with the Lord, our self-control grows greater.

James 3:2 *Those who control their tongues can also control themselves in every other way.*

Before we speak to our children, it's important that we think about what we want to say. Self-control often starts with taming the tongue.

Romans 8:5 *Those who are dominated by the sinful nature think about sinful things, but those who are controlled by the Holy Spirit think about things that please the Spirit.*

The best self-control is really "Spirit control."

Galatians 5:22-23 *But when the Holy Spirit controls our lives, he will produce this kind of fruit in us: love, joy, peace . . . and self-control.*

Self-control is one of the primary marks of the Holy Spirit's presence and activity in our lives.

PROMISE FROM GOD: 2 Peter 1:8 *The more you grow like this, the more you will become productive and useful in your knowledge of our Lord Jesus Christ.*

OOPERATION

See also UNITY

How can I teach my children to work together as a team?

Psalm 133:1 *How wonderful it is, how pleasant, when brothers live together in harmony!*

We should teach our children to cooperate with others and to always seek unity. We can help them realize that disagreements should never become personal attacks.

How can I help my children to cooperate with someone they don't get along with?

Proverbs 27:17 *As iron sharpens iron, a friend sharpens a friend.*

Disagreements can produce a positive result—to introduce new ideas that may challenge and stimulate our thinking.

1 Corinthians 1:10 *Now, dear brothers and sisters, I appeal to you by the authority of the Lord Jesus Christ to stop arguing among yourselves. Let there be real harmony so there won't be divisions in the church. I plead with you to be of one mind, united in thought and purpose.*

Loving confrontation is different from argumentativeness. Conflict is inevitable; when it arises, true cooperation seeks the highest good for all. Working together meets many of our needs.

Mark 6:7 *And he called his twelve disciples together and sent them out two by two.*

Ecclesiastes 4:12 *A triple-braided cord is not easily broken.*

Teaming up with another can give strength and encouragement when times get rough.

Ephesians 4:12-13 *Build up the church, the body of Christ, until we come to such unity in our faith.*
Cooperation exercises our spiritual gifts, allowing us to be productive for God and to mature in our faith.

How can I cooperate with God in my role as a parent?

Psalm 37:5 *Commit everything you do to the LORD. Trust him, and he will help you.*

PROMISE FROM GOD: Psalm 34:14-15 *Work hard at living in peace with others. The eyes of the LORD watch over those who do right.*

CRISIS

How should I respond to crisis?

Jonah 2:1-2 *Then Jonah prayed to the LORD his God from inside the fish. He said, "I cried out to the LORD in my great trouble, and he answered me. I called to you from the world of the dead, and LORD, you heard me!"*

Psalm 130:1-2 *From the depths of despair, O LORD, I call for your help. Hear my cry, O Lord. Pay attention to my prayer.*

When we reach the end of our rope, we must call upon the Lord, for our weaknesses are times for his strength; our crises are his opportunities.

Psalm 57:1 *Have mercy on me, O God, have mercy! I look to you for protection. I will hide beneath the shadow of your wings until this violent storm is past.*

When a crisis leaves me vulnerable and exposed, I will seek the merciful protective covering of the Lord himself.

Psalm 28:7 *The LORD is my strength, my shield from every danger. I trust in him with all my heart. He helps me, and my heart is filled with joy. I burst out in songs of thanksgiving.*

A crisis may leave us wondering, "Who can I trust?" Crisis should leave us assured, "I can always trust the Lord." That is cause for praise and thanksgiving.

Psalm 119:143 *As pressure and stress bear down on me, I find joy in your commands.*

When crises seek to undermine me, I should look to God's Word to undergird me.

Where is God in my time of crisis?

Jonah 1:17 *Now the LORD had arranged for a great fish to swallow Jonah. And Jonah was inside the fish for three days and three nights.*

Jonah 2:6 *I sank down to the very roots of the mountains. I was locked out of life and imprisoned in the land of the dead. But you, O LORD my God, have snatched me from the yawning jaws of death!*

Psalm 40:2 *He lifted me out of the pit of despair, out of the mud and the mire. He set my feet on solid ground and steadied me as I walked along.*

Psalm 46:1-2 *God is our refuge and strength, always ready to help in times of trouble. So we will not fear.*

Psalm 69:33 *For the LORD hears the cries of his needy ones; he does not despise his people who are oppressed.*

Romans 8:35 *Can anything ever separate us from Christ's love? Does it mean he no longer loves us if we have trouble or calamity, or are persecuted, or are hungry or cold or in danger or threatened with death?*

We need not pray for the Lord to be with us in times of crisis. He is already with us. Instead we need to pray that we might recognize his presence and then depend on him for help.

How can I help others in their times of crisis?

Proverbs 27:10 *Never abandon a friend—either yours or your father's. Then in your time of need, you won't have to ask your relatives for assistance. It is better to go to a neighbor than to a relative who lives far away.*

Proverbs 31:8 *Speak up for those who cannot speak for themselves; ensure justice for those who are perishing.*

1 Corinthians 9:22 *When I am with those who are oppressed, I share their oppression so that I might bring them to Christ. Yes, I try to find common ground with everyone so that I might bring them to Christ.*

Titus 3:14 *For our people should not have unproductive lives. They must learn to do good by helping others who have urgent needs.*

When others face crises, I need to be there with them. The power of my personal presence may comfort them more than the eloquence of my words.

PROMISE FROM GOD: Psalm 46:1 *God is our refuge and strength, always ready to help in times of trouble.*

CRITICISM

How should I respond to criticism?

Proverbs 12:16-18 *A wise person stays calm when insulted. An honest witness tells the truth; a false witness tells lies. Some people make cutting remarks, but the words of the wise bring healing.*

If you are criticized, stay calm, and don't lash back. Evaluate whether the criticism is coming from a person with a reputation for telling the truth or lies. Ask yourself if the criticism is meant to heal or hurt.

Ecclesiastes 7:5 *It is better to be criticized by a wise person than to be praised by a fool!*

Measure criticism according to the stature of the person who is giving it.

1 Corinthians 4:4-5 *My conscience is clear, but that isn't what matters. It is the Lord himself who will examine me and decide.*

Always work to maintain a clear conscience by being honest and trustworthy. This allows you to shrug off criticism that you know is unjustified.

1 Peter 4:14 *Be happy if you are insulted for being a Christian, for then the glorious Spirit of God will come upon you.*

Consider it a privilege to be criticized for your faith in God. God has special blessings for those who patiently endure this kind of criticism.

CRITICISM

Should we be careful about criticizing others?

Romans 14:10 *So why do you condemn another Christian? Remember, each of us will stand personally before the judgment seat of God.*

James 4:11 *If you criticize each other and condemn each other, then you are criticizing and condemning God's law.*

Constructive criticism should always be a welcome and wholesome gift if given in a spirit of love. But we have no right to give deprecating criticism of another, for that is trying to be a judge over that person, and God alone is our judge.

How do we administer criticism when we feel it must be given?

John 8:7 *Let those who have never sinned throw the first stones!*

Romans 2:1 *When you say they are wicked and should be punished, you are condemning yourself, for you do these very same things.*

Before criticizing another, take an inventory of your own sins and shortcomings so that you can approach the person with understanding and humility.

1 Corinthians 13:5 *Love does not demand its own way. Love is not irritable, and it keeps no record of when it has been wronged.*

Constructive criticism should always be offered in love, to build up. And criticism should always be responded to in love as well.

PROMISE FROM GOD: Proverbs 12:18 *Some people make cutting remarks, but the words of the wise bring healing.*

$\mathscr{D}$ECISIONS

What must I do to make good decisions?

Psalm 25:4 *Show me the path where I should walk,*
O LORD; point out the right road for me to follow.
Follow God's direction.

Luke 6:12-13 *One day soon afterward Jesus went to a*
mountain to pray, and he prayed to God all night. At day-
break he called together all of his disciples and chose twelve
of them to be apostles.
Saturate your life with prayer.

Romans 2:18 *Yes, you know what he wants; you know*
right from wrong because you have been taught his law.
Consult God's Word for God's wisdom.

Psalm 37:30 *The godly offer good counsel; they know what*
is right from wrong.

Proverbs 12:15 *Fools think they need no advice, but the*
wise listen to others.
Listen to godly counsel.

Proverbs 18:15 *Intelligent people are always open to new*
ideas. In fact, they look for them.
Be open to good advice.

How does God guide our decision making?

Psalm 25:12 *Who are those who fear the LORD? He will*
show them the path they should choose.

Proverbs 4:5 *Learn to be wise, and develop good judg-*
ment. Don't forget or turn away from my words.

Philippians 2:13 *For God is working in you, giving you the desire to obey him and the power to do what pleases him.*

We should pray for God to give us the desire to obey him and seek his guidance. When we obey, he will guide.

What is the danger of indecision?

Isaiah 42:20 *You see and understand what is right but refuse to act on it. You hear, but you don't really listen.*

James 1:5-8 *If you need wisdom—if you want to know what God wants you to do—ask him, and he will gladly tell you. . . . But when you ask him, be sure that you really expect him to answer, for a doubtful mind is as unsettled as a wave of the sea that is driven and tossed by the wind. People like that should not expect to receive anything from the Lord. They can't make up their minds. They waver back and forth in everything they do.*

Indecision is really a decision not to make a decision. Indecision regarding matters of faith can slowly but persistently draw us away from God.

PROMISE FROM GOD: Proverbs 3:6 *Seek his will in all you do, and he will direct your paths.*

DEPRESSION

What causes depression?

1 Samuel 16:14 *Now the Spirit of the LORD had left Saul, and the LORD sent a tormenting spirit that filled him with depression and fear.*

If you depart from the Lord, and then he departs from you, depression can move easily into the vacant room in your heart.

Job 30:16 *And now my heart is broken. Depression haunts my days.*
A broken heart is ripe for depression.

Ecclesiastes 4:8 *This is the case of a man who is all alone, without a child or a brother, yet who works hard to gain as much wealth as he can. But then he asks himself, "Who am I working for? Why am I giving up so much pleasure now?" It is all so meaningless and depressing.*
If you spend your life pursuing meaningless things, you are bound to get depressed as you realize that what you are doing has little lasting value.

Jeremiah 20:14, 18 *I curse the day I was born! May the day of my birth not be blessed. . . . Why was I ever born? My entire life has been filled with trouble, sorrow, and shame.*
Depression likes to keep company with trouble, sorrow, and shame.

Proverbs 13:12 *Hope deferred makes the heart sick, but when dreams come true, there is life and joy.*
A heart without hope is a heart ripe for depression.

How should I handle depression?

Psalm 143:7 *Come quickly, LORD, and answer me, for my depression deepens. Don't turn away from me, or I will die.*
The Lord's strong presence in our lives is the best cure for depression. But with the Lord's help, we may also seek the best medical help and ask him to use it to heal us.

How does God bring healing to those who are depressed?

Psalm 10:17 *LORD, you know the hopes of the helpless. Surely you will listen to their cries and comfort them.*

Psalm 23:4 *Even when I walk through the dark valley of death, I will not be afraid, for you are close beside me. Your rod and your staff protect and comfort me.*

Psalm 34:18 *The LORD is close to the brokenhearted; he rescues those who are crushed in spirit.*

Psalm 147:3 *He heals the brokenhearted, binding up their wounds.*

Matthew 5:4 *God blesses those who mourn, for they will be comforted.*

The power of the Lord's presence, coupled with the sensitivity of his listening ear, can bring healing and comfort.

How can I help someone who is depressed?

2 Corinthians 1:4 *He comforts us in all our troubles so that we can comfort others. When others are troubled, we will be able to give them the same comfort God has given us.*

Romans 12:15 *When others are happy, be happy with them. If they are sad, share their sorrow.*

Proverbs 25:20 *Singing cheerful songs to a person whose heart is heavy is as bad as stealing someone's jacket in cold weather or rubbing salt in a wound.*

PROMISE FROM GOD: Matthew 11:28 *Then Jesus said, "Come to me, all of you who are weary and carry heavy burdens, and I will give you rest."*

$\mathcal{D}$ISAPPOINTMENT

What disappoints God?

Genesis 6:5-6 *Now the LORD observed the extent of the people's wickedness, and he saw that all their thoughts were consistently and totally evil. So the LORD was sorry he had ever made them. It broke his heart.*

Wickedness or evil

Hebrews 3:17-18 *And who made God angry for forty years? Wasn't it the people who sinned, whose bodies fell in the wilderness? And to whom was God speaking when he vowed that they would never enter his place of rest? He was speaking to those who disobeyed him.*

Sin, disobedience, unbelief, and lack of trust

Malachi 1:8-10 *"When you give blind animals as sacrifices, isn't that wrong? And isn't it wrong to offer animals that are crippled and diseased? . . . I am not at all pleased with you," says the LORD Almighty, "and I will not accept your offerings."*

Giving God less than our best

2 Timothy 2:4 *As Christ's soldier, do not let yourself become tied up in the affairs of this life, for then you cannot satisfy the one who has enlisted you in his army.*

Letting other things in our lives overshadow the Lord

Is there a way to avoid or minimize disappointment?

Haggai 1:6, 9 *You have planted much but harvested little. . . . Why? Because my house lies in ruins, says the LORD Almighty, while you are all busy building your own fine houses.*

Put God first.

DISAPPOINTMENT

Psalm 22:5 *You heard their cries for help and saved them. They put their trust in you and were never disappointed.*

Psalm 34:2 *I will boast only in the LORD; let all who are discouraged take heart.*

1 Peter 2:6 *As the Scriptures express it, "I am placing a stone in Jerusalem, a chosen cornerstone, and anyone who believes in him will never be disappointed."*

Put your faith, trust, and expectations in the Lord.

Galatians 6:9 *Don't get tired of doing what is good. Don't get discouraged and give up, for we will reap a harvest of blessing at the appropriate time.*

Maintain the joy of doing God's good work.

Ecclesiastes 10:8-9 *When you dig a well, you may fall in. When you demolish an old wall, you could be bitten by a snake. When you work in a quarry, stones might fall and crush you! When you chop wood, there is danger with each stroke of your ax! Such are the risks of life.*

To live the great adventure of life, you must accept the risks that come with the adventure.

Galatians 6:4 *Be sure to do what you should, for then you will enjoy the personal satisfaction of having done your work well, and you won't need to compare yourself to anyone else.*

Do what is right, and the satisfaction of a job well done will minimize disappointment.

PROMISE FROM GOD: Psalm 55:22 *Give your burdens to the LORD, and he will take care of you.*

ISCIPLINE

See also PUNISHMENT

What are the benefits of discipline?

Psalm 119:67 *I used to wander off until you disciplined me; but now I closely follow your word.*

Discipline can keep us following God's Word more closely.

Proverbs 6:23 *These commands and this teaching are a lamp to light the way ahead of you. The correction of discipline is the way to life.*

Hebrews 12:11 *No discipline is enjoyable while it is happening—it is painful! But afterward there will be a quiet harvest of right living for those who are trained in this way.*

Discipline promotes right living.

How does God discipline his children?

Hebrews 12:7 *As you endure this divine discipline, remember that God is treating you as his own children. Whoever heard of a child who was never disciplined?*

As a loving father

Deuteronomy 8:5 *You should realize that just as a parent disciplines a child, the LORD your God disciplines you to help you.*

Psalm 119:75 *I know, O LORD, that your decisions are fair; you disciplined me because I needed it.*

As we need it

Jeremiah 31:18 *You disciplined me severely, but I deserved it. I was like a calf that needed to be trained for*

the yoke and plow. Turn me again to you and restore me, for you alone are the LORD my God.
As we deserve it

How should I discipline my children?

Proverbs 13:24 *If you refuse to discipline your children, it proves you don't love them; if you love your children, you will be prompt to discipline them.*
With love

Proverbs 19:18 *Discipline your children while there is hope. If you don't, you will ruin their lives.*
When they need it—before it is too late

Colossians 3:21 *Fathers, don't aggravate your children. If you do, they will become discouraged and quit trying.*
Without causing aggravation and discouragement

Hebrews 12:10 *Our earthly fathers disciplined us for a few years, doing the best they knew how. But God's discipline is always right and good for us because it means we will share in his holiness.*
With whatever wisdom we have!

≡PROMISE FROM GOD: Psalm 94:12 *Happy are those whom you discipline, LORD.*

DISTRACTIONS

How do I deal with distractions?

Matthew 19:13-15 *Some children were brought to Jesus so he could lay his hands on them and pray for them. The disciples told them not to bother him. But Jesus said, "Let the children come to me. Don't stop them! For the Kingdom of Heaven belongs to such as these." And he put his hands on their heads and blessed them before he left.*

Mark 10:17 *As he was starting out on a trip, a man came running up to Jesus, knelt down, and asked, "Good Teacher, what should I do to get eternal life?"*

Distractions happened all the time in Jesus' ministry. The difference in the way he handled distractions and the way we do is that he just worked the distractions right into the main focus of his life! In other words, Jesus didn't see them as distractions, just as opportunities to save the lost!

Acts 16:29-32 *Trembling with fear, the jailer called for lights and ran to the dungeon and fell down before Paul and Silas. He brought them out and asked, "Sirs, what must I do to be saved?" They replied, "Believe on the Lord Jesus and you will be saved, along with your entire household." Then they shared the word of the Lord with him.*

Paul in jail—circumstance distraction. . . . Some of us would have looked at a jail sentence as a definite distraction to our mission from God. Not Paul and Silas! Their mission just continued in the jail cell!

How can God use distractions?

Exodus 3:1-4 *One day Moses was tending the flock of his father-in-law, Jethro. . . . Suddenly, the angel of the LORD appeared to him as a blazing fire in a bush. Moses was amazed because the bush was engulfed in flames, but it didn't burn up. . . . "Why isn't that bush burning up? I must go over to see this." When the LORD saw that he had caught Moses' attention, God called to him from the bush.*

Moses was just out on an ordinary day doing his ordinary job! God used the bush, a definite distraction, to get Moses' attention.

Acts 9:3-4 *As he was nearing Damascus on this mission, a brilliant light from heaven suddenly beamed down upon him! He fell to the ground and heard a voice saying to him, "Saul! Saul! Why are you persecuting me?"*

God can refocus our sights on his ways, distracting us from our ways. Paul was on his mission to persecute Christians when God got his attention with a distraction that was even harder to ignore than Moses' bush and changed the course of his whole life (and the lives of many others!).

PROMISE FROM GOD: Hebrews 12:13 *Mark out a straight path for your feet. Then those who follow you, though they are weak and lame, will not stumble and fall but will become strong.*

DIVORCE

What are some ways to prevent divorce?

Ephesians 5:24-25 *As the church submits to Christ, so you wives must submit to your husbands in everything. And you husbands must love your wives with the same love Christ showed the church.*

1 Thessalonians 5:11 *Encourage each other and build each other up.*

Couples who love each other with the kind of love Christ showed when he died for us, who seek to please one another, and who encourage each other and build up one another—these are the couples who will likely remain together in a happy marriage. The format is simple, but the fulfillment takes some doing! Never let your marriage become a marriage of convenience.

What does the Bible say about divorce?

Malachi 2:14-16 *You cry out, "Why has the LORD abandoned us?" I'll tell you why! Because the LORD witnessed the vows you and your wife made to each other on your wedding day. . . . But you have been disloyal. . . . Didn't the LORD make you one? In body and spirit you are his. . . . So guard yourself; remain loyal. . . . "For I hate divorce!" says the LORD.*

God sees divorce as wrong because it is the breaking of a binding commitment. One or both spouses have made a conscious decision to be unfaithful.

Matthew 19:3 *Some Pharisees came and tried to trap him. . . . "Should a man be allowed to divorce his wife for any reason?"*

There is a wide range of interpretation concerning this passage, with wide application to specific situations. The Old Testament provides specific rules concerning divorce and limited remarriage in special cases (Deuteronomy 24:1-4), while at the same time making it clear that divorce is not God's intention (Malachi 2:14-16). The New Testament also makes it clear that divorce is wrong (Matthew 5:31-32; 1 Corinthians 7:10-11), while allowing for limited exceptions as Jesus mentions in this passage.

PROMISE FROM GOD: Matthew 19:6 *Since they are no longer two but one, let no one separate them, for God has joined them together.*

$\mathcal{E}$MOTIONS

How can I best handle my emotions?

Proverbs 4:23 *Above all else, guard your heart, for it affects everything you do.*

Guard your heart, for it is the wellspring of your emotions. Don't put little bandages on your emotions when you can control the source.

Job 7:11 *I cannot keep from speaking. I must express my anguish. I must complain in my bitterness.*

Keep an open dialog with the Lord and others you trust so that you are not covering up your emotions.

Ezra 3:12-13 *Many of the older priests, Levites, and other leaders remembered the first Temple, and they wept aloud when they saw the new Temple's foundation. The others, however, were shouting for joy. The joyful shouting and weeping mingled together in a loud commotion that could be heard far in the distance.*

A single event can produce multiple emotions. While you celebrate a rainstorm for your crops, others may mourn because it rained on their parade. Try to understand that the feelings of others may be quite different from yours, even over the same event.

Ephesians 4:23 *There must be a spiritual renewal of your thoughts and attitudes.*

Romans 13:14 *Let the Lord Jesus Christ take control of you, and don't think of ways to indulge your evil desires.*

Let Christ control you, and then he will help you control your emotions.

How do I experience life's most positive emotions?

Galatians 5:22-23 *When the Holy Spirit controls our lives, he will produce this kind of fruit in us: love, joy, peace, patience, kindness, goodness, faithfulness, gentleness, and self-control. Here there is no conflict with the law.*

Romans 8:6 *If your sinful nature controls your mind, there is death. But if the Holy Spirit controls your mind, there is life and peace.*

Life's most positive and healthy emotions are the fruit of the Spirit of God being lived out in our lives.

PROMISE FROM GOD: Galatians 5:22-23 *When the Holy Spirit controls our lives, he will produce this kind of fruit in us: love, joy, peace, patience, kindness, goodness, faithfulness, gentleness, and self-control.*

ENCOURAGEMENT

When do we most need encouragement?

Numbers 13:30 *But Caleb tried to encourage the people as they stood before Moses. "Let's go at once to take the land,"* he said. *"We can certainly conquer it!"*

When we stand at life's crossroads

Isaiah 35:3 *With this news, strengthen those who have tired hands, and encourage those who have weak knees.*

When we are tired and weak

ENCOURAGEMENT

1 Thessalonians 5:14 *Encourage those who are timid. Take tender care of those who are weak.*
When we feel that life's challenges are stronger than we are

Titus 2:6 *In the same way, encourage the young men to live wisely in all they do.*
As we move through life's stages

Deuteronomy 3:28 *But commission Joshua and encourage him, for he will lead the people across the Jordan. He will give them the land you now see before you.*
When we are thrust into a place of leadership

2 Chronicles 35:2 *Josiah also assigned the priests to their duties and encouraged them in their work at the Temple of the LORD.*
When God has a job for us to do

How does God encourage me?

1 Kings 19:4-6 *Then he went on alone into the desert, traveling all day. He sat down under a solitary broom tree and prayed that he might die. "I have had enough, LORD," he said. . . . But as he was sleeping, an angel touched him and told him, "Get up and eat!" He looked around and saw some bread baked on hot stones and a jar of water!*
He meets my needs at just the right time.

Psalm 138:3 *When I pray, you answer me; you encourage me by giving me the strength I need.*
He gives me strength when I ask.

Psalm 119:25, 28 *I lie in the dust, completely discouraged; revive me by your word. I weep with grief; encourage me by your word.*

Romans 15:4 *Such things were written in the Scriptures long ago to teach us. They give us hope and encouragement as we wait patiently for God's promises.*

He's given his written word to revive me and offer me hope.

Matthew 9:2 *Some people brought to him a paralyzed man on a mat. Seeing their faith, Jesus said to the paralyzed man, "Take heart, son! Your sins are forgiven."*

Matthew 9:22 *Jesus turned around and said to her, "Daughter, be encouraged! Your faith has made you well." And the woman was healed at that moment.*

He forgives my sins.

Hebrews 12:5 *And have you entirely forgotten the encouraging words God spoke to you, his children? He said, "My child, don't ignore it when the Lord disciplines you, and don't be discouraged when he corrects you."*

Even his discipline is an encouragement, for I know it is for my ultimate good.

How can I be an encouragement to others?

1 Samuel 23:16 *Jonathan went to find David and encouraged him to stay strong in his faith in God.*

By helping friends keep a close relationship with God

Ephesians 4:29 *Don't use foul or abusive language. Let everything you say be good and helpful, so that your words will be an encouragement to those who hear them.*

By making sure everything you say is kind and uplifting

2 Chronicles 32:8 *"He may have a great army, but they are just men. We have the LORD our God to help us and to fight our battles for us!" These words greatly encouraged the people.*

By reminding people what God can do, and wants to do, for and through them.

2 Chronicles 30:22 *Hezekiah encouraged the Levites for the skill they displayed as they served the LORD.*
By complimenting others for a job well done

Titus 1:9 *He must have a strong and steadfast belief in the trustworthy message he was taught; then he will be able to encourage others with right teaching and show those who oppose it where they are wrong.*
By sharing God's instruction and correction

Proverbs 15:30 *A cheerful look brings joy to the heart; good news makes for good health.*
By a smile!

PROMISE FROM GOD: **2 Thessalonians 2:16-17** *May our Lord Jesus Christ and God our Father comfort your hearts and give you strength in every good thing you do and say.*

ENVY

What causes envy?

Genesis 26:12-14 *That year Isaac's crops were tremendous! Soon the Philistines became jealous of him.*

James 4:2 *You want what you don't have, so you scheme and kill to get it. You are jealous for what others have, and you can't possess it, so you fight and quarrel to take it away from them.*

People become jealous when they see someone who has more than they have or something they do not have.

Daniel 6:3-4 *Daniel soon proved himself more capable than all the other administrators and princes. Because of his great ability, the king made plans to place him over the entire empire. Then the other administrators and princes began searching for some fault in the way Daniel was handling his affairs.*

People become jealous when they see someone do a better job than they are doing, or perhaps even better than they want to do.

Psalm 73:3 *I envied the proud when I saw them prosper despite their wickedness.*

It is easy to envy an evil person who prospers more than the righteous.

Ecclesiastes 4:4 *Then I observed that most people are motivated to success by their envy of their neighbors. But this, too, is meaningless, like chasing the wind.*

Trying to keep up with others is both the cause of envy and the fruit of envy.

What is the result of envy?

Job 5:2 *Surely resentment destroys the fool, and jealousy kills the simple.*

Psalm 37:8 *Stop your anger! Turn from your rage! Do not envy others—it only leads to harm.*

Proverbs 14:30 *A relaxed attitude lengthens life; jealousy rots it away.*

Proverbs 27:4 *Anger is cruel, and wrath is like a flood, but who can survive the destructiveness of jealousy?*

James 3:16 *Wherever there is jealousy and selfish ambition, there you will find disorder and every kind of evil.*

Envy unchecked will eventually destroy you.

What do I do about my feelings of envy?

Psalm 37:1, 7 *Don't worry about the wicked. Don't envy those who do wrong. . . . Be still in the presence of the LORD, and wait patiently for him to act.*

We can respond to envy by trying to get what we don't have or by allowing bitterness to take hold in our lives. Or we can patiently wait for God to act in our lives in the way that is best for us. And isn't what God wants for us better than what we want for ourselves?

Proverbs 24:19-20 *Do not fret because of evildoers; don't envy the wicked. For the evil have no future; their light will be snuffed out.*

Why envy sinners; all they can inherit is judgment. Desire what the Lord has in store for you.

John 21:20-22 *Peter turned around and saw the disciple Jesus loved following them—the one who had leaned over to Jesus during supper and asked, "Lord, who among us will betray you?" Peter asked Jesus, "What about him, Lord?" Jesus replied, "If I want him to remain alive until I return, what is that to you? You follow me."*

Get your marching orders from God straight, and don't worry about any of the other soldiers! Let God work out his plan in others just as he is working out his plan in you.

PROMISE FROM GOD: **Psalm 37:8-9** *Do not envy others—it only leads to harm. For the wicked will be destroyed, but those who trust in the LORD will possess the land.*

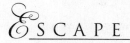
ESCAPE

What do I do when I have a desire to escape?

Psalm 139:7 *I can never escape from your spirit! I can never get away from your presence!*

Jeremiah 23:24 *"Can anyone hide from me? Am I not everywhere in all the heavens and earth?" asks the LORD.*
Recognize that you cannot escape from God.

Psalm 32:7 *You are my hiding place; you protect me from trouble. You surround me with songs of victory.*

Psalm 46:1 *God is our refuge and strength, always ready to help in times of trouble.*

Psalm 57:1 *Have mercy on me, O God, have mercy! I look to you for protection. I will hide beneath the shadow of your wings until this violent storm is past.*

Nahum 1:7 *The LORD is good. When trouble comes, he is a strong refuge. And he knows everyone who trusts in him.*
When we have to escape, it should be into the arms of our loving God.

How does God provide ways of escape?

Genesis 7:7 *[Noah] went aboard the boat to escape— he and his wife and his sons and their wives.*

Genesis 19:17 *"Run for your lives!" the angels warned. "Do not stop anywhere in the valley. And don't look back! Escape to the mountains, or you will die."*

Exodus 14:21 *Then Moses raised his hand over the sea, and the LORD opened up a path through the water with a strong east wind. The wind blew all that night, turning the seabed into dry land.*

He provides literal, physical ways to escape.

Proverbs 14:27 *Fear of the LORD is a life-giving fountain; it offers escape from the snares of death.*

2 Peter 2:20 *People escape from the wicked ways of the world by learning about our Lord and Savior Jesus Christ.*

He helps us escape from evil into a relationship with him.

1 Corinthians 10:13 *God is faithful. He will keep the temptation from becoming so strong that you can't stand up against it. When you are tempted, he will show you a way out so that you will not give in to it.*

He helps us escape from the wrong way to the right way.

PROMISE FROM GOD: Hebrews 6:18 *God has given us both his promise and his oath. These two things are unchangeable because it is impossible for God to lie. Therefore, we who have fled to him for refuge can take new courage, for we can hold on to his promise with confidence.*

EXAMPLE

As a mother, what kind of example should I be for my children?

Titus 2:7 *And you yourself must be an example to them by doing good deeds of every kind.*

Strive to be the kind of example your children will want to follow.

1 Thessalonians 1:5 *And you know that the way we lived among you was further proof of the truth of our message.*

A good role model is responsible and accountable.

Jeremiah 1:10 *Today I appoint you to stand up against nations and kingdoms.*

A good role model not only does what is right but speaks out against wrong.

Hebrews 5:12 *You have been Christians a long time now, and you ought to be teaching others.*

A good role model teaches others about God's ways.

1 Timothy 4:12 *Don't let anyone think less of you because you are young. Be an example to all believers in what you teach, in the way you live, in your love, your faith, and your purity.*

Age need not be a barrier to being a good role model.

Matthew 5:13 *You are the salt of the earth. But what good is salt if it has lost its flavor?*

A good role model influences others for good rather than being easily influenced by evil.

Hosea 6:3 *Let us press on to know him!*

Being a good role model doesn't mean you are perfect, but that you are striving for maturity.

Matthew 20:28 *For even I, the Son of Man, came here not to be served but to serve others.*

Being a good role model doesn't make you a celebrity; it makes you a servant.

Who can I look to as my role model?

1 Corinthians 11:1 *And you should follow my example, just as I follow Christ's.*

In other people, we find assorted characteristics we would like to follow. In Jesus Christ, we find all of the characteristics we would like to follow. When you have a question about what to do, ask yourself what Jesus would have done.

PROMISE FROM GOD: Proverbs 28:2 *With wise and knowledgeable leaders, there is stability.*

EXPECTATIONS

Are there expectations that I should have?

Proverbs 11:23 *The godly can look forward to happiness, while the wicked can expect only wrath.*

2 Corinthians 3:8, 12 *Shouldn't we expect far greater glory when the Holy Spirit is giving life? . . . Since this new covenant gives us such confidence, we can be very bold.*

Hebrews 10:26-27 *Dear friends, if we deliberately continue sinning after we have received a full knowledge of the truth, there is no other sacrifice that will cover these sins. There will be nothing to look forward to but the terrible expectation of God's judgment and the raging fire that will consume his enemies.*

If we live for God, we can expect a glorious future, but if we live in rebellion against God, we can expect judgment.

Romans 5:3-5 *We can rejoice, too, when we run into problems and trials, for we know that they are good for us—they help us learn to endure. And endurance develops strength of character in us, and character strengthens our confident expectation of salvation. And this expectation will not disappoint us. For we know how dearly God loves us, because he has given us the Holy Spirit to fill our hearts with his love.*

Those who have trusted in Christ for salvation should expect that God will save them.

Luke 2:25 *There was a man named Simeon who lived in Jerusalem. He was a righteous man and very devout. He was filled with the Holy Spirit, and he eagerly expected the Messiah to come and rescue Israel.*

We should live in eager expectation of Christ's coming.

James 1:5-7 *If you need wisdom—if you want to know what God wants you to do—ask him, and he will gladly tell you. He will not resent your asking. But when you ask him, be sure that you really expect him to answer, for a doubtful mind is as unsettled as a wave of the sea that is driven and tossed by the wind. People like that should not expect to receive anything from the Lord.*

When we pray, we should be confident and expect that God will answer us.

Are there expectations that I shouldn't have?

Psalm 10:6 *They say to themselves, "Nothing bad will ever happen to us! We will be free of trouble forever!"*

Isaiah 33:1 *You expect others to respect their promises to you, while you betray your promises to them. Now you, too, will be betrayed and destroyed!*

Ezekiel 33:13 *When I tell righteous people that they will live, but then they sin, expecting their past righteousness to save them, then none of their good deeds will be remembered. I will destroy them for their sins.*

It is erroneous to expect that we can live in sin and never suffer the consequences.

Ecclesiastes 10:8-9 *When you dig a well, you may fall in. When you demolish an old wall, you could be bitten by a snake. When you work in a quarry, stones might fall and crush you! When you chop wood, there is danger with each stroke of your ax! Such are the risks of life.*

We should not expect life to be free from danger.

2 Corinthians 11:7 *Did I do wrong when I humbled myself and honored you by preaching God's Good News to you without expecting anything in return?*

We should not expect to be rewarded by others for serving God and obeying him.

PROMISE FROM GOD: 1 Peter 1:3-4 *All honor to the God and Father of our Lord Jesus Christ, for it is by his boundless mercy that God has given us the privilege of being born again. Now we live with a wonderful expectation because Jesus Christ rose again from the dead. For God has reserved a priceless inheritance for his children. It is kept in heaven for you, pure and undefiled, beyond the reach of change and decay.*

FAILURE

When I have failed, how do I get past it and go on?

1 Kings 8:33-34 *If your people Israel are defeated by their enemies because they have sinned against you, and if they turn to you and call on your name and pray to you here in this Temple, then hear from heaven and forgive their sins and return them to this land you gave their ancestors.*

Turning to God in repentance and trust is the best response we can have to our own failure.

Proverbs 24:16 *They may trip seven times, but each time they will rise again. But one calamity is enough to lay the wicked low.*

Micah 7:8 *Though I fall, I will rise again. Though I sit in darkness, the LORD himself will be my light.*

2 Corinthians 4:9 *We are hunted down, but God never abandons us. We get knocked down, but we get up again and keep going.*

The best response to failure is to get up again, with the hope that God gives us through faith.

How do I keep from failing?

Numbers 14:22 *Not one of these people will ever enter that land. They have seen my glorious presence and the miraculous signs I performed both in Egypt and in the wilderness, but again and again they tested me by refusing to listen.*

Joshua 7:7-12 *Then Joshua cried out, "Sovereign LORD, why did you bring us across the Jordan River if you are going to let the Amorites kill us? If only we had been content to stay on the other side! Lord, what am I to say, now that Israel has fled from its enemies? . . . But the LORD said to Joshua, "Get up! Why are you lying on your face like this? Israel has sinned and broken my covenant! . . . That is why the Israelites are running from their enemies in defeat."*

Hebrews 4:6   *God's rest is there for people to enter. But those who formerly heard the Good News failed to enter because they disobeyed God.*

We can prevent failure by listening to God and doing what he says.

Matthew 7:24-25   *Anyone who listens to my teaching and obeys me is wise, like a person who builds a house on solid rock. Though the rain comes in torrents and the floodwaters rise and the winds beat against that house, it won't collapse, because it is built on rock.*

By listening to Christ and his instructions, we can avoid failure.

Isaiah 42:23   *Will not even one of you apply these lessons from the past and see the ruin that awaits you?*

We can avoid failure if we learn from the mistakes of the past.

PROMISE FROM GOD: Psalm 37:23-24   *The steps of the godly are directed by the LORD. He delights in every detail of their lives. Though they stumble, they will not fall, for the LORD holds them by the hand.*

FAIRNESS

Fairness is a big issue for my children. What's the goal of fairness?

Matthew 7:12 *Do for others what you would like them to do for you.*

Isaiah 33:15 *The ones who can live here are those who are honest and fair.*

Being fair is making sure that right prevails, that people are not unjustly treated. It indicates we are thinking more about others than ourselves and that we have a sensitivity to their needs. It demonstrates a sense of justice that does not want to see evil or sin win. It is an inner desire for integrity and an outward desire to build up the self-worth of others. It is to be like Christ.

What about "getting even"?

Proverbs 24:29 *And don't say, "Now I can pay them back for all their meanness to me! I'll get even!"*

Seeking justice against evil is fair and right; getting even is revenge.

What's the difference between fairness and justice?

Isaiah 10:1 *Destruction is certain for the unjust judges, for those who issue unfair laws.*

Romans 2:5-6 *For there is going to come a day of judgment when God, the just judge of all the world, will judge all people according to what they have done.*

Fairness is playing by the rules; justice is holding other people accountable when they don't.

Does God play favorites?

Psalm 7:11 *God is a judge who is perfectly fair.*
If God gave us what we deserved, none of us would make it to heaven, for the Bible says that all people have sinned against God (Rom. 3:23). God is not only fair by offering us another way to heaven, he is merciful by giving it to us free. All we need to do is accept it (Rom. 6:23).

Ecclesiastes 9:11 *The fastest runner doesn't always win the race, and the strongest warrior doesn't always win the battle. The wise are often poor, and the skillful are not necessarily wealthy.*

John 3:16 *Everyone who believes in him will not perish but have eternal life.*
God does not promise us equality of things here on earth, but he does promise that all have an equal chance of eternal life in heaven, where there will be no more adverse circumstances.

How can I treat all my children fairly?

Zechariah 8:16 *But this is what you must do: Tell the truth to each other. Render verdicts in your courts that are just and that lead to peace.*
We need to treat people equally as much as possible. However, in the occasional circumstance when this is impossible, we still need to be equal in the way we love and value them.

PROMISE FROM GOD: Psalm 103:6 *The LORD gives righteousness and justice to all who are treated unfairly.*

FAITH

Why should I have faith in God?

Isaiah 25:9 *This is the LORD, in whom we trusted. Let us rejoice in the salvation he brings!*

John 5:24 *I assure you, those who listen to my message and believe in God who sent me have eternal life.*

Faith is the only way to get to heaven. It is the only doorway to eternal life. If God created eternity, then only through God can we get there.

Hebrews 11:1 *What is faith? It is the confident assurance that what we hope for is going to happen.*

Faith gives us hope.

How does faith in God affect my life?

Genesis 15:6 *And Abram believed the LORD, and the LORD declared him righteous because of his faith.*

Romans 3:24-25 *God in his gracious kindness declares us not guilty. . . . We are made right with God when we believe that Jesus shed his blood, sacrificing his life for us.*

Sin breaks our relationship with God because it is rebellion against God. A holy God cannot live with unholy people. But when we accept Jesus as Savior and ask him to forgive our sins, this simple act of faith makes us righteous in God's sight.

Isaiah 26:3 *You will keep in perfect peace all who trust in you.*

Faith in God brings peace of mind and heart because we know that we belong to him, and we know that one day all pain and suffering will end.

Romans 8:5 *Those who are controlled by the Holy Spirit think about things that please the Spirit.*

1 Corinthians 12:1 *I will write about the special abilities the Holy Spirit gives to each of us.*

Galatians 5:22 *When the Holy Spirit controls our lives, he will produce this kind of fruit in us: love, joy, peace, patience, kindness, goodness, faithfulness.*

Faith is inviting God's Holy Spirit to live within us. It is not just an act of the mind, but it taps us into the very resources of God so that we have the power to live in an entirely new way. If God himself is living within us, our lives should be dramatically changed.

When I'm struggling in my Christian life and have doubts, does it mean I have less faith?

Genesis 15:8 *Abram replied, "O Sovereign LORD, how can I be sure that you will give it to me?"*

Matthew 11:2-3 *John the Baptist . . . sent his disciples to ask Jesus, "Are you really the Messiah we've been waiting for?"*

2 Peter 1:1-9 *He has given us all of his rich and wonderful promises. . . . So make every effort to apply the benefits of these promises to your life.*

Many people in the Bible whom we consider to be "pillars of faith" had moments of doubt. The key is to never give up on our faith and to always ask if, over time, our lives have been moving closer to or farther away from God. Even during moments of doubt, you must invest the effort and discipline to allow your faith to grow.

PROMISE FROM GOD: Acts 16:31 *They replied, "Believe on the Lord Jesus and you will be saved, along with your entire household."*

FAMILY

What is family? How does the Bible define it?

Genesis 2:24 *This explains why a man leaves his father and mother and is joined to his wife, and the two are united into one.*

Ephesians 2:19 *You are members of God's family.*

James 1:18 *In his goodness he chose to make us his own children.*

The Bible talks about both an earthly family, made up of husband and wife and usually children, and the family of God, which is all believers united together by the bond of faith.

1 Chronicles 9:1 *All Israel was listed in the genealogical record in The Book of the Kings of Israel.*

The Bible lists several genealogies, all recorded by family units, showing the family as central and fundamental to the development of people and of nations.

Proverbs 6:20-23 *My son, obey your father's commands, and don't neglect your mother's teaching.*

Nowhere can truth be more effectively taught and modeled than in the family.

Joshua 24:15 *As for me and my family, we will serve the LORD.*

The family is one of God's greatest resources for communicating truth and effecting change in any community. This change is directly related to the family's spiritual commitment and zeal.

Psalm 127:3 *Children are a gift from the LORD; they are a reward from him.*

Children are a wonderful blessing.

What is my responsibility to my family?

Deuteronomy 6:7 *Repeat [God's commands] again and again to your children. Talk about them when you are at home.*

Proverbs 22:6 *Teach your children to choose the right path, and when they are older, they will remain upon it.*

To give them spiritual training and explain the gospel of Jesus to them

Exodus 10:2 *You will be able to tell wonderful stories to your children and grandchildren about the marvelous things I am doing.*

2 Timothy 1:5 *I know that you sincerely trust the Lord, for you have the faith of your mother, Eunice, and your grandmother, Lois.*

To share spiritual experiences with them and remind them of their spiritual heritage

Ephesians 6:4 *Bring them up with the discipline and instruction approved by the Lord.*

Titus 2:4-5 *These older women must train the younger women to love their husbands and their children . . . to take care of their homes.*

To love them, and discipline them when necessary. To teach them proper conduct. To be a good role model

Proverbs 31:27 *She carefully watches all that goes on in her household and does not have to bear the consequences of laziness.*

To provide for them

1 Samuel 3:13 *I have warned him continually that judgment is coming for his family, because his sons are blaspheming God and he hasn't disciplined them.*

1 Kings 1:6 *Now his father . . . had never disciplined him at any time, even by asking, "What are you doing?"*

Proverbs 29:15 *To discipline and reprimand a child produces wisdom, but a mother is disgraced by an undisciplined child.*

Neglecting to teach your children spiritual truths and neglecting discipline have tragic consequences.

PROMISE FROM GOD: Psalm 102:28 *The children of your people will live in security. Their children's children will thrive in your presence.*

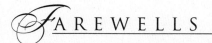

FAREWELLS

How should I bid others farewell? What can make a farewell easier?

Ruth 1:8-9 *On the way, Naomi said to her two daughters-in-law, "Go back to your mothers' homes instead of coming with me. And may the LORD reward you for your kindness to your husbands and to me. May the LORD bless you with the security of another marriage."*

Put the other person's needs ahead of my own needs.

1 Samuel 20:42 *At last Jonathan said to David, "Go in peace, for we have made a pact in the LORD's name. We have entrusted each other and each other's children into the LORD's hands forever." Then David left, and Jonathan returned to the city.*

Entrust the other person into God's care while you are gone.

Genesis 24:58-60 *They called Rebekah. "Are you willing to go with this man?" they asked her. And she replied, "Yes, I will go." So they said good-bye to Rebekah and sent her away with Abraham's servant and his men. The woman who had been Rebekah's childhood nurse went along with her. They blessed her with this blessing as she parted: "Our sister, may you become the mother of many millions! May your descendants overcome all their enemies."*

Don't hold on; allow the departure—with a blessing!

2 Timothy 1:4 *I long to see you again, for I remember your tears as we parted. And I will be filled with joy when we are together again.*

Anticipate the next meeting.

What should be my perspective on farewells caused by death?

Ecclesiastes 8:8 *None of us can hold back our spirit from departing.*

Realize that death is inevitable for all of us.

Isaiah 25:8 *He will swallow up death forever! The Sovereign LORD will wipe away all tears. He will remove forever all insults and mockery against his land and people. The LORD has spoken!*

Realize God's ultimate power over death.

Matthew 25:46 *They will go away into eternal punishment, but the righteous will go into eternal life.*

Realize that there is life after death.

Revelation 7:17 *The Lamb who stands in front of the throne will be their Shepherd. He will lead them to the springs of life-giving water. And God will wipe away all their tears.*

Realize the eternal quality of life after death for the Christian.

PROMISE FROM GOD: John 14:27-28 *I am leaving you with a gift—peace of mind and heart. . . . Remember what I told you: I am going away, but I will come back to you again.*

FORGIVENESS

Do I have to forgive others who hurt me?

Matthew 6:14-15 *If you forgive those who sin against you, your heavenly Father will forgive you. But if you refuse to forgive others, your Father will not forgive your sins.*

Mark 11:25 *When you are praying, first forgive anyone you are holding a grudge against, so that your Father in heaven will forgive your sins, too.*

We will receive God's forgiveness only when we are willing to forgive others who have wronged us.

Matthew 18:21-22 *Then Peter came to him and asked, "Lord, how often should I forgive someone who sins against me? Seven times?" "No!" Jesus replied, "seventy times seven!"*

Just as God forgives us without limit, we should forgive others without counting how many times.

Luke 17:3-4 *If another believer sins, rebuke him; then if he repents, forgive him. Even if he wrongs you seven times a day and each time turns again and asks forgiveness, forgive him.*

Forgiveness doesn't have to be cheap.

Luke 23:34 *Jesus said, "Father, forgive these people, because they don't know what they are doing."*

Jesus forgave those who mocked him and killed him.

Colossians 3:13 *You must make allowance for each other's faults and forgive the person who offends you. Remember, the Lord forgave you, so you must forgive others.*

1 Peter 3:9 *Don't repay evil for evil. Don't retaliate when people say unkind things about you. Instead, pay them back with a blessing. That is what God wants you to do, and he will bless you for it.*

God wants us to respond to others' sins by blessing them.

Is there a limit to how much God will forgive me?

Isaiah 1:18 *"Come now, let us argue this out," says the LORD. "No matter how deep the stain of your sins, I can remove it. I can make you as clean as freshly fallen snow. Even if you are stained as red as crimson, I can make you as white as wool."*

Joel 2:32 *Anyone who calls on the name of the LORD will be saved.*

No matter how sinful and disobedient we have been, we can receive God's forgiveness by turning to him in repentance.

Psalm 86:5 *O Lord, you are so good, so ready to forgive, so full of unfailing love for all who ask your aid.*

Psalm 103:3 *He forgives all my sins and heals all my diseases.*

Ezekiel 18:22 *All their past sins will be forgotten, and they will live because of the righteous things they have done.*

God is ready to forgive us.

Matthew 18:23-27 *The Kingdom of Heaven can be compared to a king who decided to bring his accounts up to date. . . . One of his debtors was brought in who owed him millions of dollars. He couldn't pay. . . . Then the king was filled with pity for him, and he released him and forgave his debt.*

God is merciful toward us even though our debt is so great.

Luke 24:47 *With my authority, take this message of repentance to all the nations, beginning in Jerusalem: "There is forgiveness of sins for all who turn to me."*

Ephesians 1:7 *He is so rich in kindness that he purchased our freedom through the blood of his Son, and our sins are forgiven.*

Colossians 1:14 *God has purchased our freedom with his blood and has forgiven all our sins.*

God will forgive every sin because Christ has already paid the penalty for all sin by his death.

Mark 3:29 *Anyone who blasphemes against the Holy Spirit will never be forgiven. It is an eternal sin.*

Those who harden themselves against God's Spirit and reject him utterly will never experience his forgiveness.

⋑PROMISE FROM GOD: 1 John 1:9 *If we confess our sins to him, he is faithful and just to forgive us and to cleanse us from every wrong.*

FRIENDSHIP

What is the mark of true friendship?

Proverbs 17:17 *A friend is always loyal, and a brother is born to help in time of need.*

1 Samuel 18:3 *Jonathan made a special vow to be David's friend.*

Some friendships are fleeting, and some are lasting. True friendships are glued together with bonds of loyalty and commitment. They remain intact, despite changing external circumstances.

What gets in the way of friendships?

1 Samuel 18:9-11 *From that time on Saul kept a jealous eye on David. . . . Saul, who had a spear in his hand, suddenly hurled it at David.*

Jealousy is the great dividing force of friendships. Envy over what a friend has will soon turn to anger and bitterness, causing you to separate yourself from the one you truly cared for.

Psalm 41:9 *Even my best friend, the one I trusted completely . . . has turned against me.*

When respect or reverence is seriously damaged, even the closest friendship is at risk.

2 Samuel 13:11 *As she was feeding him, he grabbed her and demanded, "Come to bed with me."*

Friendships are destroyed when boundaries are violated.

Genesis 50:17, 21 *"So we . . . beg you to forgive us."
. . . "No, don't be afraid. Indeed, I myself will take care of you."*

Forgiveness restores broken relationships.

What do I do when I'm having trouble making friends?

Job 19:19 *My close friends abhor me. Those I loved have turned against me.*

John 5:7 *I have no one to help me into the pool.*

We all go through times when it seems our friends have deserted us.

John 15:15 *I no longer call you servants. . . . Now you are my friends.*

Hebrews 13:5 *I will never fail you. I will never forsake you.*

The first thing we must do is remember that God is our constant friend and will never leave us.

Ephesians 4:32 *Instead, be kind to each other, tender-hearted, forgiving one another, just as God through Christ has forgiven you.*

Acts of kindness and generosity attract others to you.

PROMISE FROM GOD: Matthew 18:20 *Where two or three gather together because they are mine, I am there among them.*

FRUSTRATION

What frustrates God?

Psalm 78:40-42 *Oh, how often they rebelled against him in the desert and grieved his heart in the wilderness. Again and again they tested God's patience and frustrated the Holy One of Israel. They forgot about his power and how he rescued them from their enemies.*

Hosea 6:4 *O Israel and Judah, what should I do with you?" asks the LORD. "For your love vanishes like the morning mist and disappears like dew in the sunlight.*

It is frustrating to God to send out unending streams of love, mercy, and forgiveness to his people, only to see them dam these streams of blessings and keep their souls a spiritual desert.

How can I best deal with frustration?

Ecclesiastes 1:8 *Everything is so weary and tiresome! No matter how much we see, we are never satisfied. No matter how much we hear, we are not content.*

Ecclesiastes 2:20 *I turned in despair from hard work. It was not the answer to my search for satisfaction in this life.*

Psalm 90:14 *Satisfy us in the morning with your unfailing love, so we may sing for joy to the end of our lives.*

Acts 17:25 *Human hands can't serve his needs—for he has no needs. He himself gives life and breath to everything, and he satisfies every need there is.*

We are frustrated when we fail to let God be God or when we try to understand the reasons for everything that happens. When we let go and let God work out what is best for us, we will relieve much of our frustration.

PROMISE FROM GOD: Joshua 1:9 *I command you—be strong and courageous! Do not be afraid or discouraged. For the LORD your God is with you wherever you go.*

GENTLENESS

How is God gentle?

1 Kings 19:12 *After the earthquake there was a fire, but the LORD was not in the fire. And after the fire there was the sound of a gentle whisper.*

Psalm 18:35 *You have given me the shield of your salvation. Your right hand supports me; your gentleness has made me great.*

Psalm 103:13-14 *The LORD is like a father to his children, tender and compassionate to those who fear him. For he understands how weak we are; he knows we are only dust.*

Isaiah 42:3 *He will not crush those who are weak or quench the smallest hope.*

Although God has the power of the universe at his finger-tips, he often speaks most eloquently to us in whispers.

How did Jesus demonstrate gentleness?

Isaiah 40:11 *He will feed his flock like a shepherd. He will carry the lambs in his arms, holding them close to his heart. He will gently lead the mother sheep with their young.*

Matthew 9:36 *He felt great pity for the crowds that came, because their problems were so great and they didn't know where to go for help.*

Mark 6:34 *A vast crowd was there as he stepped from the boat, and he had compassion on them because they were like sheep without a shepherd. So he taught them many things.*

Matthew 11:28-29 *Then Jesus said, "Come to me, all of you who are weary and carry heavy burdens, and I will give you rest. Take my yoke upon you. Let me teach you, because I am humble and gentle, and you will find rest for your souls."*

We see the heart and mind of Jesus best through images like shepherding (holding us like little lambs), pitying the crowds of hurting people, lifting heavy burdens, and representing sinful people before almighty God. These are the marks of gentleness.

How can I be gentle in my life?

Genesis 33:3-4, 10 *Jacob went on ahead. As he approached his brother, he bowed low seven times before him. Then Esau ran to meet him and embraced him affectionately and kissed him. Both of them were in tears. Jacob said, "What a relief it is to see your friendly smile. It is like seeing the smile of God!"*

Give a friendly smile in tense times.

1 Peter 3:4 *You should be known for the beauty that comes from within, the unfading beauty of a gentle and quiet spirit, which is so precious to God.*

A gentle and quiet spirit has unfading beauty.

Colossians 3:12-13 *Since God chose you to be the holy people whom he loves, you must clothe yourselves with tenderhearted mercy, kindness, humility, gentleness, and patience. You must make allowance for each other's faults and forgive the person who offends you.*

Show mercy, kindness, humility, gentleness, patience, and forgiveness toward others.

James 3:17 *The wisdom that comes from heaven is . . . peace loving, gentle at all times.*

Utilize God's wisdom.

Galatians 6:1 *Dear brothers and sisters, if another Christian is overcome by some sin, you who are godly should gently and humbly help that person back onto the right path.*

Use loving guidance for those who have gone astray.

2 Timothy 2:24-25 *The Lord's servants must not quarrel but must be kind to everyone. They must be able to teach effectively and be patient with difficult people. They should gently teach those who oppose the truth. Perhaps God will change those people's hearts, and they will believe the truth.*

Use gentle words in teaching others, especially unbelievers.

Proverbs 15:1, 4 *A gentle answer turns away wrath, but harsh words stir up anger. . . . Gentle words bring life and health; a deceitful tongue crushes the spirit.*

Use words of healing and peace.

GOD'S WILL AND THE HAND OF GOD

Does God really have a plan for my life and the lives of my children?

Psalm 139:3 *You chart the path ahead of me and tell me where to stop and rest. Every moment you know where I am.*

God cares about what we do. He cares about the details of our lives because they are a barometer of the condition of our heart.

Psalm 138:8 *The LORD will work out his plans for my life.*

God's plans for us are always for good. Unknown plans can be frightening, but when the plans belong to God, we can rest assured that we can expect something marvelous.

Psalm 32:8 *The LORD says, "I will guide you along the best pathway for your life. I will advise you and watch over you."*

God definitely wants to help us follow the path that will be most pleasing to him, not the path that may be most pleasing to us.

How can I help my children to discover God's will for their lives?

Proverbs 2:3-5 *Cry out for insight and understanding. Search for them as you would for lost money or hidden treasure. Then you will understand what it means to fear the LORD.*

Teach them to look for God's will for their lives.

Isaiah 2:3 *Come, let us go up to the mountain of the LORD, to the Temple of the God of Israel. There he will teach us his ways, so that we may obey him.*

Spend time together reading God's Word.

Hosea 6:3 *Oh, that we might know the LORD! Let us press on to know him! Then he will respond to us.*

Give yourself completely to knowing his will. Seek God's will passionately, not casually.

James 1:5 *If you want to know what God wants you to do—ask him, and he will gladly tell you. He will not resent your asking.*

Proverbs 2:6 *For the LORD grants wisdom!*

1 John 5:14 *We can be confident that he will listen to us whenever we ask him for anything in line with his will.*

Pray, asking God to reveal his will to you.

Acts 21:14 *When it was clear that we couldn't persuade him, we gave up and said, "The will of the Lord be done."*

Sometimes the best way to know God's will is to let go and let God have his wonderful way, especially when it comes to our children. We may learn more about his will for us as we allow him to work out his will in our lives.

What are some of the things we know are God's will for us?

Amos 5:24 *I want to see a mighty flood of justice, a river of righteous living that will never run dry.*

God's will is that we seek justice at all times and that we do what is right.

1 Corinthians 14:1 *Let love be your highest goal.*

God's will is that we love others.

Mark 10:45 *Even I, the Son of Man, came here not to be served but to serve others.*

God's will is that we serve others, putting them above ourselves.

Exodus 20:1 *Then God instructed the people.*

God's will is that we obey his laws for living.

Galatians 5:22 *When the Holy Spirit controls our lives, he will produce this kind of fruit in us.*

God's will is that we live under the power and guidance of the Holy Spirit.

Proverbs 16:3 *Commit your work to the LORD, and then your plans will succeed.*

God's will is that we do everything as if we were doing it for him.

What do we mean by "the hand of God," and how does God work in my family?

Psalm 66:5 *Come and see what our God has done, what awesome miracles he does for his people!*

God works on behalf of his people in miraculous ways.

Deuteronomy 4:34 *Has any other god taken one nation for himself by rescuing it from another by means of trials, miraculous signs, wonders, war, awesome power, and terrifying acts? Yet that is what the LORD your God did for you in Egypt, right before your very eyes.*

God works through trials, miraculous signs, wonders, war, awesome power, and even terrifying acts.

Daniel 6:27 *He rescues and saves his people; he performs miraculous signs and wonders in the heavens and on earth. He has rescued Daniel from the power of the lions.*

God works to rescue and save his people.

Jeremiah 31:35 *It is the LORD who provides the sun to light the day and the moon and stars to light the night. It is he who stirs the sea into roaring waves. His name is the LORD Almighty.*

If the Creator can control creation, shouldn't he have control over our families?

What does God's hand bring to us?

James 1:17 *Whatever is good and perfect comes to us from God above, who created all heaven's lights.*

Everything good and perfect comes from God's hand.

Job 2:10 *Job replied, ". . . Should we accept only good things from the hand of God and never anything bad?"*

Sometimes God withdraws his hand and allows bad things to happen to good people. Why? Because his long-range eternal plans for our greater good may not fit our short-range view of comfort.

Ecclesiastes 2:24 *I decided there is nothing better than to enjoy food and drink and to find satisfaction in work. Then I realized that this pleasure is from the hand of God.*

The pleasure of God's provision transcends the pleasure of the provisions themselves. For example, it feels even better to know God gives us bread than it does to taste the bread itself.

PROMISE FROM GOD: Jeremiah 29:11 *"I know the plans I have for you," says the LORD. "They are plans for good and not for disaster, to give you a future and a hope."*

GOSSIP

Why is gossip so bad?

Leviticus 19:16 *Do not spread slanderous gossip among your people.*

Gossip is specifically forbidden by God.

Proverbs 11:13 *A gossip goes around revealing secrets, but those who are trustworthy can keep a confidence.*

Gossips make poor friends. Stay away from them. Gossips and trustworthy people work at opposite ends of the human spectrum. Trustworthy people build you up. Gossips are demolition experts, trying to tear you down.

Romans 1:29 *Their lives became full of every kind of wickedness, sin, greed, hate, envy, murder, fighting, deception, malicious behavior, and gossip.*

God catalogs gossip with greed, hate, envy, and murder.

1 Timothy 5:13 *They are likely to become lazy and spend their time gossiping . . . getting into other people's business and saying things they shouldn't.*

Gossiping often grows out of laziness. When we have nothing better to do than sit around talking about other people, then we wind up saying things we might later regret.

Matthew 7:1 *Stop judging others, and you will not be judged.*

Gossip puts us in the place of judging others. In a court of law, rumors and opinions are not allowed because they might unjustly sway the opinion of the jury. So it is when we turn our living rooms into courtrooms where we sit as judge and allow rumors and opinions to color and often damage the reputation of others who have no chance to defend themselves.

Proverbs 18:8 *What dainty morsels rumors are—but they sink deep into one's heart.*

Gossip hurts others. It also destroys your credibility if the gossip proves false.

How do I stop gossip?

Proverbs 26:20 *Fire goes out for lack of fuel, and quarrels disappear when gossip stops.*

Stop the chain of gossip with you! When you hear gossip, you can do something about it. You can decide not to spread it any further. Stop the fires of gossip from spreading beyond you.

Deuteronomy 13:14 *You must examine the facts carefully.*

If you are not sure something is gossip, you must look carefully into the matter without assuming what you have been told is true. Go to the source, and get the facts straight.

Matthew 7:12 *Do for others what you would like them to do for you.*

The Golden Rule can also be applied to our speech—"Talk about others in the same way you would like them to talk about you."

Ephesians 4:29 *Let everything you say be good and helpful, so that your words will be an encouragement to those who hear them.*

If we focus on what is good and helpful, gossip will find no foothold in our hearts.

Colossians 3:17 *Whatever you do or say, let it be as a representative of the Lord Jesus.*

If you think you may be about to gossip, ask yourself, Does the person I'm talking to need to know this? Is it true, accurate, and helpful?

PROMISE FROM GOD: 1 Peter 3:10 *For the Scriptures say, "If you want a happy life and good days, keep your tongue from speaking evil, and keep your lips from telling lies."*

GRACE

See MERCY

GRIEF AND LOSS

How can I best deal with the losses in my life?

Job 1:20-22 *Job stood up and tore his robe in grief. Then he shaved his head and fell to the ground before God. He said,*

"I came naked from my mother's womb, and I will be stripped of everything when I die. The LORD gave me everything I had, and the LORD has taken it away. Praise the name of the LORD!" In all of this, Job did not sin by blaming God.

Lamentations 3:19-23 *The thought of my suffering and homelessness is bitter beyond words. I will never forget this awful time, as I grieve over my loss. Yet I still dare to hope when I remember this: The unfailing love of the LORD never ends! By his mercies we have been kept from complete destruction. Great is his faithfulness; his mercies begin afresh each day.*

Those who know God grieve with him, where there is hope. Those who don't have God grieve without him, the source of greatest hope.

Hebrews 10:34 *You suffered along with those who were thrown into jail. When all you owned was taken from you, you accepted it with joy. You knew you had better things waiting for you in eternity.*

It is important to grieve, but recognize that our grieving is short-term. One day we will be with God in heaven, where all grief will be gone forever.

How can God help me survive life's losses?

Psalm 10:17 *LORD, you know the hopes of the helpless. Surely you will listen to their cries and comfort them.*

Psalm 30:11-12 *You have turned my mourning into joyful dancing. You have taken away my clothes of mourning and clothed me with joy, that I might sing praises to you and not be silent. O LORD my God, I will give you thanks forever!*

Psalm 102:17 *He will listen to the prayers of the destitute. He will not reject their pleas.*

Lamentations 3:32 *Though he brings grief, he also shows compassion according to the greatness of his unfailing love.*

Matthew 5:4 *God blesses those who mourn, for they will be comforted.*

2 Corinthians 1:3 *All praise to the God and Father of our Lord Jesus Christ. He is the source of every mercy and the God who comforts us.*

In times of loss, God fills us with his blessings—comfort, joy, songs of praise, thanksgiving, and mercy. When we cry out for someone to touch us, God will hold us close.

How can I help my children deal with grief?

Genesis 50:1 *Joseph threw himself on his father and wept over him.*

2 Samuel 18:33 *The king was overcome with emotion. He went up to his room over the gateway and burst into tears. And as he went, he cried, "O my son Absalom!"*

First, recognize that grief is necessary and important. We need the freedom to grieve. It is an important part of closure because it allows us to honestly express the way we feel.

Genesis 23:2-4 *There Abraham mourned and wept for her. Then, leaving her body, he went to the Hittite elders and said, ". . . Please let me have a piece of land for a burial plot."*

Participate in the process of grief. Take time to personally mourn, but also become involved in the necessary steps to bring closure to your loss. We grieve because we have had a positive experience—what we lost was important to us. Getting involved in the process of grief is a way of honoring what was meaningful.

Ecclesiastes 3:4 *A time to cry and a time to laugh. A time to grieve and a time to dance.*

Grief has its own season, but then it is time to move on to another. God wants us to wipe our tears, move on, and be redemptive to other grieving people.

Isaiah 66:13 *I will comfort you there as a child is comforted by its mother.*

2 Corinthians 1:3 *He is the source of every mercy and the God who comforts us.*

God knows we grieve, understands our sorrow, and comforts us. He does not promise to preserve us from grief, but he promises to help us through it.

Revelation 21:4 *He will remove all of their sorrows, and there will be no more death or sorrow or crying or pain.*

Take hope that there will be no more grief in heaven.

PROMISE FROM GOD: Psalm 147:3 *He heals the brokenhearted, binding up their wounds.*

HABITS

What are some of the bad habits the Bible talks about?

1 John 3:8 *When people keep on sinning, it shows they belong to the Devil.*

Sin is a habit none of us can stop completely, but a pattern of sinful living shows that we may not be serious about following God.

Exodus 8:28-32 *"All right, go ahead," Pharaoh replied. "I will let you go. . . ." But Pharaoh hardened his heart again and refused to let the people go.*

Pharaoh developed a bad habit of lying and wanting his own way. Both of these are habits we can easily slip into, but they are disastrous.

Numbers 11:1 *The people soon began to complain . . . about their hardships.*

The Israelites developed a bad habit of complaining. Regular complaining can quickly turn into bitterness.

1 Timothy 5:13 *They are likely to become lazy and spend their time gossiping.*

Too much time and too little to do can be fertile ground for bad habits. This idleness makes it easy to develop the bad habit of gossip. Here Paul was talking about widows, who had more time on their hands because the church supported them. But the principle applies to us all.

How do we deal with bad habits?

Romans 7:5 *I don't understand myself at all, for I really want to do what is right, but I don't do it. Instead, I do the very thing I hate.*

Have you ever felt this way? Paul reveals to us one of the best ways to deal with bad habits—recognize them for what they are and confess them honestly. Paul knew that he could not kick the habit of sin overnight. But he knew that, with God's help, he could make progress every day. In the same way, we may have to give up a habit in phases, one day at a time.

1 John 2:15 *Stop loving this evil world and all that it offers you.*

Sin often appears lovely and attractive. In the same way, bad habits often feel good even though we know they are ultimately bad for us. Breaking a bad habit can be hard because we are losing something we like. Understand that there may be a grieving process. But this pain over losing a bad habit brings the deeper joy that we are doing what is pleasing to God.

Colossians 3:2 *Let heaven fill your thoughts.*
We must replace a bad habit with something good.

How do we develop good habits?

Hebrews 10:25 *Let us not neglect our meeting together, as some people do.*
Meeting together as believers is a good habit because it provides necessary fellowship with other believers, it develops the habit of group Bible study, it keeps us busy when we might otherwise be slipping into bad habits, and it offers an accountability group.

Genesis 26:21-22 *Isaac's men then dug another well, but again there was a fight over it. . . . Abandoning that one, he dug another well, and the local people finally left him alone.*
Isaac pursued a habit of peace. In this case it meant staying away from the source of the conflict, the Philistines, even at great cost.

Psalm 28:7 *The LORD is my strength, my shield from every danger. I trust in him with all my heart. . . . I burst out in songs of thanksgiving.*
As a young boy, David developed the habit of talking to God, singing songs about him, and writing psalms. This helped him to trust in and follow God all his life.

PROMISE FROM GOD: Romans 8:5-6 *Those who are dominated by the sinful nature think about sinful things, but those who are controlled by the Holy Spirit think about things that please the Spirit. If your sinful nature controls your mind, there is death. But if the Holy Spirit controls your mind, there is life and peace.*

HAND OF GOD

See GOD'S WILL AND
THE HAND OF GOD

HAPPINESS

How can I bring happiness to God?

Deuteronomy 30:10 *The LORD your God will delight in you if you obey his voice and keep the commands and laws written in this Book of the Law, and if you turn to the LORD your God with all your heart and soul.*

Proverbs 11:1 *The LORD . . . delights in honesty.*

Proverbs 11:20 *The LORD . . . delights in those who have integrity.*

Proverbs 15:8 *The LORD . . . delights in the prayers of the upright.*

Proverbs 15:26 *The LORD . . . delights in pure words.*
Can we finite, sinful human beings truly bring joy and delight to the Lord, the Creator of the universe? Yes, and

it is simple, though not easy—honor him, obey him, respond to his love, seek his forgiveness, and walk daily with him.

How does God express his happiness with me?

Zephaniah 3:17 *The LORD your God has arrived to live among you. He is a mighty savior. He will rejoice over you with great gladness. With his love, he will calm all your fears. He will exult over you by singing a happy song.*

Psalm 18:19 *He led me to a place of safety; he rescued me because he delights in me.*

Psalm 149:4 *The LORD delights in his people; he crowns the humble with salvation.*

The Lord delights in saving us from our sins, guiding us in his ways, and taking daily care of us.

What is the source of true happiness?

Psalm 40:16 *May all who search for you be filled with joy and gladness. May those who love your salvation repeatedly shout, "The LORD is great!"*

Psalm 68:3 *Let the godly rejoice. Let them be glad in God's presence. Let them be filled with joy.*

Psalm 86:4 *Give me happiness, O Lord, for my life depends on you.*

Psalm 146:5 *Happy are those who have the God of Israel as their helper, whose hope is in the LORD their God.*

The Lord himself is the wellspring of true happiness. The more we love him, know him, walk with him, and become like him, the greater our happiness.

How can I bring happiness to others?

Romans 12:10 *Love each other with genuine affection, and take delight in honoring each other.*

2 Corinthians 7:13 *In addition to our own encouragement, we were especially delighted to see how happy Titus was at the way you welcomed him and set his mind at ease.*

As God is the wellspring of true happiness, so we are the conduits of that happiness to others.

PROMISE FROM GOD: Proverbs 11:23 *The godly can look forward to happiness, while the wicked can expect only wrath.*

HEALING

From what do we need to be healed?

Luke 8:42 *His only child was dying, a little girl twelve years old.*

Mark 1:40 *A man with leprosy came and knelt in front of Jesus, begging to be healed.*

We long to be healed from sickness and disease.

Isaiah 61:1 *He has sent me to comfort the brokenhearted.*

Our broken hearts need healing and restoration.

Psalm 30:11 *You have turned my mourning into joyful dancing.*

We need healing from sorrow.

Psalm 55:20 *As for this friend of mine, he betrayed me.*

We need to be healed from the pain of betrayal.

Romans 6:23 *The wages of sin is death, but the free gift of God is eternal life.*

Psalm 103:3 *He forgives all my sins.*
We need to be healed from sin.

Proverbs 17:22 *A cheerful heart is good medicine, but a broken spirit saps a person's strength.*
There is a connection between a healthy spirit and a positive attitude.

How does God heal?

2 Kings 20:7 *"Make an ointment from figs and spread it over the boil." They did this, and Hezekiah recovered!*
Through physicians and medicine

Psalm 119:93 *I will never forget your commandments, for you have used them to restore my joy and health.*

Mark 3:5 *He said to the man, "Reach out your hand." The man reached out his hand, and it became normal again!*
Through his commands

Luke 5:12-13 *"Lord," he said, "if you want to, you can make me well again." Jesus reached out and touched the man. "I want to," he said. "Be healed!"*
Through miracles

Mark 2:4-5 *They couldn't get to Jesus through the crowd, so they dug through the clay roof above his head. . . . Seeing their faith, Jesus said to the paralyzed man, "My son, your sins are forgiven."*
Through the faith of friends

Psalm 6:2 *Heal me, LORD, for my body is in agony.*

James 5:14 *Are any among you sick? They should call for the elders of the church and have them pray over them.*
Through prayer

Isaiah 38:16 *Lord, your discipline is good, for it leads to life and health.*
Through discipline

Genesis 27:41; 33:4 *Esau hated Jacob. . . . Then Esau ran to meet him and embraced him affectionately and kissed him. Both of them were in tears.*
Through time

Isaiah 53:5 *He was wounded and crushed for our sins. He was beaten that we might have peace. He was whipped, and we were healed!*
By death Christ brought us life. Through woundedness he brought us healing. By accepting our punishment, he set us free.

PROMISE FROM GOD: Malachi 4:2 *For you who fear my name, the Sun of Righteousness will rise with healing in his wings. And you will go free, leaping with joy like calves let out to pasture.*

HEALTH

How can God use my sickness in a positive way?

2 Corinthians 12:7-9 *To keep me from getting puffed up, I was given a thorn in my flesh. . . . Three different times I begged the Lord to take it away. Each time he said, "My*

gracious favor is all you need. My power works best in your weakness."

Romans 5:3-4 *We can rejoice, too, when we run into problems and trials, for we know that they are good for us—they help us learn to endure. And endurance develops strength of character in us, and character strengthens our confident expectation of salvation.*

We never welcome sickness, pain, or weakness. But we rejoice in the fruit that often comes from these things—patience, reliance on God's strength, and gratitude to God for what we do have.

How can my attitude affect my health?

Proverbs 17:22 *A cheerful heart is good medicine, but a broken spirit saps a person's strength.*

It's both a Bible truth and a fact of life—a positive, cheerful disposition has a positive impact on our health.

How do I keep my soul in good health?

1 Timothy 4:8 *Do not waste time arguing over godless ideas and old wives' tales. Spend your time and energy in training yourself for spiritual fitness. Physical exercise has some value, but spiritual exercise is much more important, for it promises a reward in both this life and the next.*

Spiritual exercise is as purposeful and strenuous as physical exercise. But the benefits of spiritual fitness last for eternity while the benefits of physical fitness last only as long as our bodies last.

PROMISE FROM GOD: 1 Timothy 4:7-8 *Physical exercise has some value, but spiritual exercise is much more important, for it promises a reward in both this life and the next.*

What kind of heart does God desire for me?

2 Kings 23:25 *Never before had there been a king like Josiah, who turned to the LORD with all his heart and soul and strength, obeying all the laws of Moses.*

God desires a devoted, obedient heart.

1 Chronicles 29:17 *I know, my God, that you examine our hearts and rejoice when you find integrity there. You know I have done all this with good motives, and I have watched your people offer their gifts willingly and joyously.*

God desires a godly heart, a heart of integrity.

Psalm 51:6, 10, 17 *But you desire honesty from the heart, so you can teach me to be wise in my inmost being. . . . Create in me a clean heart, O God. Renew a right spirit within me. . . . The sacrifice you want is a broken spirit. A broken and repentant heart, O God, you will not despise.*

God desires an honest, clean, repentant heart.

Psalm 86:11 *Teach me your ways, O LORD, that I may live according to your truth! Grant me purity of heart, that I may honor you.*

Matthew 5:8 *God blesses those whose hearts are pure, for they will see God.*

God desires a pure heart.

How can I change my heart to be the way God wants it?

2 Chronicles 12:7 *When the LORD saw their change of heart, he gave this message to Shemaiah: "Since the people*

have humbled themselves, I will not completely destroy them and will soon give them some relief."
Humble yourself before God.

Ezekiel 18:31 *Put all your rebellion behind you, and get for yourselves a new heart and a new spirit.*
Turn away from all sin, rebellion against God, and rejection of God—and turn to God.

Ezekiel 36:26 *I will give you a new heart with new and right desires, and I will put a new spirit in you. I will take out your stony heart of sin and give you a new, obedient heart.*
Let God give you a new heart in tune with him.

Hebrews 9:14 *Just think how much more the blood of Christ will purify our hearts from deeds that lead to death so that we can worship the living God. For by the power of the eternal Spirit, Christ offered himself to God as a perfect sacrifice for our sins.*
Let Christ's sacrifice purify your heart.

How do I guard and protect my heart?

Proverbs 4:23 *Above all else, guard your heart, for it affects everything you do.*

2 Chronicles 19:9 *These were his instructions to them: "You must always act in the fear of the LORD, with integrity and with undivided hearts."*

Proverbs 23:19 *My child, listen and be wise. Keep your heart on the right course.*

1 John 5:21 *Dear children, keep away from anything that might take God's place in your hearts.*

Ephesians 3:17 I pray that Christ will be more and more at home in your hearts as you trust in him. May your roots go down deep into the soil of God's marvelous love.

Keeping God at the center of your heart prevents anything else from invading it.

PROMISE FROM GOD: *Proverbs 4:23 Above all else, guard your heart, for it affects everything you do.*

HOME

How can I establish my home the way God wants it?

Psalm 127:1 Unless the LORD builds a house, the work of the builders is useless.

Proverbs 24:3-4 A house is built by wisdom and becomes strong through good sense. Through knowledge its rooms are filled with all sorts of precious riches and valuables.

Through God's Word I find God's wisdom and God's ways for my life and for my home.

How can I experience God's blessing on my home?

Proverbs 3:33 The curse of the LORD is on the house of the wicked, but his blessing is on the home of the upright.

Ezekiel 44:30 The first of the ripe fruits and all the gifts brought to the LORD will go to the priests. The first samples of each grain harvest and the first of your flour must also be given to the priests so the LORD will bless your homes.

1 Timothy 5:4 *If she has children or grandchildren, their first responsibility is to show godliness at home and repay their parents by taking care of them. This is something that pleases God very much.*

Invite the Lord into your home, and he will pour out his blessings on your home.

What are some of my responsibilities in my home?

Deuteronomy 11:19-20 *Teach [God's words] to your children. Talk about them when you are at home and when you are away on a journey, when you are lying down and when you are getting up again. Write them on the doorposts of your house and on your gates.*

Psalm 101:2 *I will be careful to live a blameless life— when will you come to my aid? I will lead a life of integrity in my own home.*

Proverbs 31:27 *She carefully watches all that goes on in her household and does not have to bear the consequences of laziness.*

As I live before other family members, I must exhibit godly role modeling—with industry, integrity, faithfulness in sharing God's Word and God's ways, purity of walk, and abundance of loving service.

≣**PROMISE FROM GOD**: Proverbs 3:33 *The curse of the LORD is on the house of the wicked, but his blessing is on the home of the upright.*

OPE

Where does hope come from?

Psalm 39:7 *And so, Lord, where do I put my hope? My only hope is in you.*

The Lord himself is the source of hope because he determines our future.

Why should I trust God as my hope?

Hebrews 6:18-19 *God has given us both his promise and his oath. These two things are unchangeable because it is impossible for God to lie. Therefore, we who have fled to him for refuge can take new courage, for we can hold on to his promise with confidence. This confidence is like a strong and trustworthy anchor for our souls. It leads us through the curtain of heaven into God's inner sanctuary.*

Hebrews 10:23 *Without wavering, let us hold tightly to the hope we say we have, for God can be trusted to keep his promise.*

1 Peter 1:21 *Through Christ you have come to trust in God. And because God raised Christ from the dead and gave him great glory, your faith and hope can be placed confidently in God.*

God cannot lie because he *is* truth. God, therefore, cannot break his promises. His word stands forever. God must be trusted as our hope because he alone conquered death by raising Christ from the dead.

Where can I go to reinforce my hope?

Romans 15:4 *Such things were written in the Scriptures long ago to teach us. They give us hope and encouragement as we wait patiently for God's promises.*

Psalm 119:43, 74, 81, 114, 147 *Do not snatch your word of truth from me, for my only hope is in your laws. . . . May all who fear you find in me a cause for joy, for I have put my hope in your word. . . . I faint with longing for your salvation; but I have put my hope in your word. . . . You are my refuge and my shield; your word is my only source of hope. . . . I rise early, before the sun is up; I cry out for help and put my hope in your words.*

Each day I can visit God's Word and have my hope renewed and reinforced. His Word never fails or wavers.

PROMISE FROM GOD: Psalm 130:7 *Hope in the LORD; for with the LORD there is unfailing love and an overflowing supply of salvation.*

HOSPITALITY

How should I show hospitality to others?

Genesis 19:2 *"My lords," he said, "come to my home to wash your feet, and be my guests for the night. You may then get up in the morning as early as you like and be on your way again."*

Genesis 24:32 *The man went home with Laban, and Laban unloaded the camels, gave him straw to bed them down, fed them, and provided water for the camel drivers to wash their feet.*

1 Peter 4:9 *Cheerfully share your home with those who need a meal or a place to stay.*

The basics of good hospitality—a place to stay and food to eat—can't almost all of us offer these simple acts of kindness toward others?

To whom should I be hospitable?

Romans 12:13 *When God's children are in need, be the one to help them out. And get into the habit of inviting guests home for dinner or, if they need lodging, for the night.*
Other Christians

3 John 1:5 *Dear friend, you are doing a good work for God when you take care of the traveling teachers who are passing through, even though they are strangers to you.*
God's workers—those in ministry

Hebrews 13:2 *Don't forget to show hospitality to strangers, for some who have done this have entertained angels without realizing it!*
Strangers

Isaiah 58:7 *I want you to share your food with the hungry and to welcome poor wanderers into your homes. Give clothes to those who need them, and do not hide from relatives who need your help.*
The hungry, poor, needy—and don't forget your relatives.

Luke 14:12-14 *He turned to his host. "When you put on a luncheon or a dinner," he said, "don't invite your friends, brothers, relatives, and rich neighbors. For they will repay you by inviting you back. Instead, invite the poor, the crippled, the lame, and the blind. Then at the resurrection of the godly, God will reward you for inviting those who could not repay you."*
Those who cannot repay you

PROMISE FROM GOD: Hebrews 13:2 *Don't forget to show hospitality to strangers, for some who have done this have entertained angels without realizing it!*

HUMILITY

What is true humility?

Zephaniah 3:12 *Those who are left will be the lowly and the humble, for it is they who trust in the name of the LORD.*

Humility is not thinking too highly of yourself.

Matthew 18:4 *Therefore, anyone who becomes as humble as this little child is the greatest in the Kingdom of Heaven.*

Humility is childlikeness.

Titus 3:2 *They must not speak evil of anyone, and they must avoid quarreling. Instead, they should be gentle and show true humility to everyone.*

Humility is gentleness.

Psalm 51:3-4 *I recognize my shameful deeds—they haunt me day and night. Against you, and you alone, have I sinned; I have done what is evil in your sight. You will be proved right in what you say, and your judgment against me is just.*

Humility is willingness to confess sin.

How was God's Son humble?

Zechariah 9:9 *Rejoice greatly, O people of Zion! Shout in triumph, O people of Jerusalem! Look, your king is coming to you. He is righteous and victorious, yet he is humble, riding on a donkey—even on a donkey's colt.*

Jesus was King of kings, yet in his royal procession he rode on a donkey.

Philippians 2:5-11 *Your attitude should be the same that Christ Jesus had. Though he was God, he did not demand and cling to his rights as God. He made himself nothing; he took the humble position of a slave and appeared in human form. And in human form he obediently humbled himself even further by dying a criminal's death on a cross. Because of this, God raised him up to the heights of heaven and gave him a name that is above every other name, so that at the name of Jesus every knee will bow, in heaven and on earth and under the earth, and every tongue will confess that Jesus Christ is Lord, to the glory of God the Father.*

Jesus was God, yet he made himself nothing and suffered death on the cross for us.

Hebrews 2:9 *What we do see is Jesus, who "for a little while was made lower than the angels" and now is "crowned with glory and honor" because he suffered death for us. Yes, by God's grace, Jesus tasted death for everyone in all the world.*

Jesus had all the glory and honor, but for our sakes he died so that we could be saved and have eternal life with him.

Matthew 11:29 *Take my yoke upon you. Let me teach you, because I am humble and gentle, and you will find rest for your souls.*

Jesus is the ultimate role model of gentleness and humility.

How does God respond to the humble?

Psalm 69:32 *The humble will see their God at work and be glad. Let all who seek God's help live in joy.*

God gives joy to the humble.

Psalm 18:27 *You rescue those who are humble, but you humiliate the proud.*

God rescues the humble.

Psalm 138:6 *Though the LORD is great, he cares for the humble, but he keeps his distance from the proud.*

God takes care of the humble.

Psalm 147:6 *The LORD supports the humble, but he brings the wicked down into the dust.*

God supports the humble.

Isaiah 29:19 *The humble will be filled with fresh joy from the LORD. Those who are poor will rejoice in the Holy One of Israel.*

God fills the humble with fresh joy.

PROMISE FROM GOD: Matthew 23:12 *Those who exalt themselves will be humbled, and those who humble themselves will be exalted.*

HUSBANDS

What are some ways I can meet my husband's needs?

Psalm 45:11 *For your royal husband delights in your beauty; honor him, for he is your lord.*

I can honor my husband.

1 Peter 3:5 *That is the way the holy women of old made themselves beautiful. They trusted God and accepted the authority of their husbands.*

I can accept my husband's authority.

Proverbs 31:11 *Her husband can trust her, and she will greatly enrich his life.*

I can be trustworthy.

1 Corinthians 7:34 *The married woman must be concerned about her earthly responsibilities and how to please her husband.*

I can think of ways to please him.

How can I best help my husband if he does not know Jesus Christ as his Savior and Lord?

1 Corinthians 7:13-16 *If a Christian woman has a husband who is an unbeliever, and he is willing to continue living with her, she must not leave him. For the Christian wife brings holiness to her marriage, and the Christian husband brings holiness to his marriage. Otherwise, your children would not have a godly influence, but now they are set apart for him. . . . You wives must remember that your husbands might be converted because of you.*

1 Peter 3:1 *In the same way, you wives must accept the authority of your husbands, even those who refuse to accept the Good News. Your godly lives will speak to them better than any words. They will be won over.*

Godly, loving role modeling is the best way to witness to an unbelieving mate.

PROMISE FROM GOD: Proverbs 12:4 *A worthy wife is her husband's joy and crown.*

Even though we've adopted a child, I still long to give birth. Does God understand this?

Genesis 30:1-2 *When Rachel saw that she wasn't having any children, she became jealous of her sister. "Give me children, or I'll die!" she exclaimed to Jacob. Jacob flew into a rage. "Am I God?" he asked. "He is the only one able to give you children!"*

Proverbs 30:15-16 *There are three other things—no, four! —that are never satisfied: the grave, the barren womb, the thirsty desert, the blazing fire.*

How can I deal with the tension and pain caused by infertility?

Isaiah 40:31 *Those who wait on the Lord will find new strength.*

God's love for us is greater than anything we could ever imagine.

Philippians 4:6-7 *Don't worry about anything; instead, pray about everything. Tell God what you need, and thank him for all he has done. If you do this, you will experience God's peace, which is far more wonderful than the human mind can understand.*

How can I accept God's timing?

Genesis 16:1-2; 21:2 *But Sarai, Abram's wife, had no children. So Sarai took her servant, an Egyptian woman named Hagar, and gave her to Abram so she could bear his children. "The LORD has kept me from having any children,"*

Sarai said to Abram. "Go and sleep with my servant. Perhaps I can have children through her."... [Later] Sarah became pregnant, and she gave a son to Abraham in his old age. It all happened at the time God had said it would.

Psalm 62:1, 5, 8 *I wait quietly before God, for my salvation comes from him.... I wait quietly before God, for my hope is in him.... O my people, trust in him at all times. Pour out your heart to him, for God is our refuge.*

Isaiah 30:18 *The LORD still waits for you to come to him so he can show you his love and compassion. For the LORD is a faithful God. Blessed are those who wait for him to help them.*

Isaiah 64:4 *Since the world began, no ear has heard, and no eye has seen a God like you, who works for those who wait for him!*

Lamentations 3:25-26 *The LORD is wonderfully good to those who wait for him and seek him. So it is good to wait quietly for salvation from the LORD.*

Sometimes God says yes when we pray. Sometimes he says no. Sometimes he wants us to wait. And sometimes we must remember that God is God and we are human, and perhaps we should not understand everything about his ways. We can accept God's timing best when we accept God as God.

Is it wrong to continue to plead to God for children?

Genesis 25:21 *Isaac pleaded with the LORD to give Rebekah a child because she was childless. So the LORD answered Isaac's prayer, and his wife became pregnant with twins.*

Genesis 30:22-24 *Then God remembered Rachel's plight and answered her prayers by giving her a child. She became pregnant and gave birth to a son. "God has removed my shame," she said. And she named him Joseph, for she said, "May the LORD give me yet another son."*

Psalm 5:3 *Listen to my voice in the morning, LORD. Each morning I bring my requests to you and wait expectantly.*

As long as you have hope, pray. As long as you believe in miracles, pray. As long as you believe in God, pray. Then let God be God. Let him do what he knows is best.

PROMISE FROM GOD: Romans 8:39 *Nothing in all creation will ever be able to separate us from the love of God that is revealed in Christ Jesus our Lord.*

INSIGNIFICANCE

How can I cope with feelings of insignificance?

Psalm 8:4-5 *What are mortals that you should think of us, mere humans that you should care for us? For you made us only a little lower than God, and you crowned us with glory and honor.*

Matthew 10:29-31 *Not even a sparrow, worth only half a penny, can fall to the ground without your Father knowing it. And the very hairs on your head are all numbered. So don't be afraid; you are more valuable to him than a whole flock of sparrows.*

The Creator of the universe considers you significant in his sight.

INSIGNIFICANCE

Psalm 119:37 *Turn my eyes from worthless things, and give me life through your word.*

Although I may feel insignificant at times, I must remember that God himself gives me life through his Word.

How can I be useful to God since I am so insignificant?

1 Corinthians 1:26-29 *Remember, dear brothers and sisters, that few of you were wise in the world's eyes, or powerful, or wealthy when God called you. Instead, God deliberately chose things the world considers foolish in order to shame those who think they are wise. And he chose those who are powerless to shame those who are powerful. God chose things despised by the world, things counted as nothing at all, and used them to bring to nothing what the world considers important, so that no one can ever boast in the presence of God.*

Significance in the eyes of the world may be insignificance in God's eyes. Insignificance in the world's eyes may be significance in God's eyes. God takes joy in using people the world considers "insignificant" to accomplish marvelous things for his kingdom.

What are some of the most significant things in life?

1 Corinthians 13:2-3 *Without love I would be no good to anybody. . . . If I didn't love others, I would be of no value whatsoever.*

Love for God and love for others

Acts 20:24 *My life is worth nothing unless I use it for doing the work assigned me by the Lord Jesus—the work of telling others the Good News about God's wonderful kindness and love.*

Serving the Lord

Philippians 3:8 Yes, everything else is worthless when compared with the priceless gain of knowing Christ Jesus my Lord. I have discarded everything else, counting it all as garbage, so that I may have Christ.

Knowing Christ personally

PROMISE FROM GOD: Psalm 8:5 *You made us only a little lower than God, and you crowned us with glory and honor.*

INTERRUPTIONS

See DISTRACTIONS

INTIMACY

What is my responsibility as well as my pleasure regarding sexual intimacy?

1 Corinthians 7:3 *The husband should not deprive his wife of sexual intimacy, which is her right as a married woman, nor should the wife deprive her husband.*

Sexual intimacy is reserved for marriage, and sexual intimacy is a mutual responsibility and pleasure for both partners. One should not deprive the other of this privilege except by mutual agreement.

What must I do to experience an intimate relationship with God?

Genesis 5:24 *He enjoyed a close relationship with God throughout his life. Then suddenly, he disappeared because God took him.*

I must walk with God—daily and consistently.

Genesis 6:9 *This is the history of Noah and his family. Noah was a righteous man, the only blameless man living on earth at the time. He consistently followed God's will and enjoyed a close relationship with him.*

I must live the way God wants me to live—daily and consistently.

Psalm 27:8 *My heart has heard you say, "Come and talk with me." And my heart responds, "LORD, I am coming."*

Psalm 145:18 *The LORD is close to all who call on him, yes, to all who call on him sincerely.*

I must talk with God—daily and consistently.

James 4:8 *Draw close to God, and God will draw close to you. Wash your hands, you sinners; purify your hearts, you hypocrites.*

I must stay close to God and purify my heart before him— daily and consistently.

Exodus 34:14 *You must worship no other gods, but only the LORD, for he is a God who is passionate about his relationship with you.*

I must worship God only—daily and consistently.

Matthew 22:37 *Jesus replied, "'You must love the Lord your God with all your heart, all your soul, and all your mind.'"*

I must love God completely—daily and consistently.

Romans 5:11 *Now we can rejoice in our wonderful new relationship with God—all because of what our Lord Jesus Christ has done for us in making us friends of God.*
I must rejoice in God through Christ—daily and consistently.

PROMISE FROM GOD: 1 Chronicles 28:9
If you seek him, you will find him.

KINDNESS

Why should we be kind to one another?

Ephesians 4:32 *Be kind to each other, tenderhearted, forgiving one another, just as God through Christ has forgiven you.*
We should be kind because God has been kind to us and commands us to be kind to others.

Matthew 7:12 *Do for others what you would like them to do for you.*
We are kind because we want others to be kind to us.

Ruth 2:10-12 *"Why are you being so kind to me?" she asked. . . . Boaz replied, "I also know about the love and kindness you have shown your mother-in-law."*
Kindness is never lost; it keeps on going from person to person until it returns to you.

How can I become kind to others?

Galatians 5:22 *When the Holy Spirit controls our lives, he will produce this kind of fruit in us: . . . kindness.*
Kindness is a fruit planted in our lives by the Holy Spirit.

1 Corinthians 13:4 *Love is patient and kind.*
From the fountains of love flow the rivers of kindness.
It is impossible to be truly kind unless we are first truly
loving.

Luke 6:35 *Love your enemies! Do good to them! Lend
to them! And don't be concerned that they might not repay.*
Kindness is based on the loving heart of the giver, not the
loving heart of the recipient.

How has God shown kindness to us?

Titus 3:4-5 *God our Savior showed us his kindness and
love. He saved us, not because of the good things we did, but
because of his mercy. He washed away our sins.*

**How do we show God our gratitude for his kindness
to us?**

Psalm 92:2 *It is good to proclaim your unfailing love
in the morning, your faithfulness in the evening.*
Do you remember daily to thank and praise the Lord for
his kindness and faithfulness?

⇛**PROMISE FROM GOD:** Matthew 10:42 *If you
give even a cup of cold water to one of the least of my
followers, you will surely be rewarded.*

ℒEADERSHIP

**What qualities do I need to be a good leader for my
children?**

Nehemiah 7:2 *I gave the responsibility of governing*

Jerusalem to my brother Hanani, . . . for he was a faithful man who feared God more than most.

Good leaders show faithfulness and reverence.

Matthew 20:26 *Whoever wants to be a leader among you must be your servant.*

Good leaders have a servant's heart.

2 Chronicles 32:20 *Then King Hezekiah and the prophet Isaiah . . . cried out in prayer to God in heaven.*

A good leader has a heart for prayer.

1 Chronicles 21:8 *Then David said to God, "I have sinned greatly and shouldn't have taken the census."*

Good leaders accept responsibility for their actions.

1 Corinthians 3:11 *For no one can lay any other foundation than the one we already have—Jesus Christ.*

Good leaders keep their eyes on Jesus.

Daniel 6:10 *He prayed three times a day, just as he had always done.*

The words and actions of a good leader are consistent. Daniel was vocal about his faith in God, even in a pagan land, and his actions backed that up.

Joshua 1:9 *Be strong and courageous! . . . For the LORD your God is with you wherever you go.*

Good leaders show courage based on the assurance of God's presence.

John 3:30 *He must become greater and greater, and I must become less and less.*

Good leaders do not emphasize themselves.

1 John 4:1 *Dear friends, do not believe everyone who claims to speak by the Spirit.*

2 John 1:10 *If someone comes to your meeting and does not teach the truth about Christ, don't . . . encourage him in any way.*

Good leaders recognize false teaching and boldly combat it.

Micah 3:1 *Listen, you leaders of Israel! You are supposed to know right from wrong.*

Good leaders are consumed with doing what is right.

Hebrews 6:1 *Let us go on instead and become mature in our understanding.*

Good leaders demonstrate maturity, both in their actions and in their knowledge of God's Word.

Proverbs 12:15 *Fools think they need no advice, but the wise listen to others.*

Good leaders have others who hold them accountable.

What is our responsibility toward our leaders?

Hebrews 13:17 *Obey your spiritual leaders and do what they say. Their work is to watch over your souls.*

Romans 13:1-5 *Obey the government, for God is the one who put it there.*

Work with leaders rather than against them to effect change.

How can I teach my children to respond to the leaders in their lives?

1 Thessalonians 5:12-13 *Honor those who are your leaders in the Lord's work. . . . Think highly of them and give them your wholehearted love because of their work.*

Honor them.

Exodus 17:12 *They stood on each side, holding up his hands until sunset.*

Encourage them.

Hebrews 13:18-19 *Pray for us. . . . I especially need your prayers right now.*

Pray for them.

Romans 14:10 *Why do you condemn another Christian? Why do you look down on another Christian?*

Don't be quick to criticize.

2 Samuel 12:1, 7 *So the LORD sent Nathan the prophet to tell David this story: . . . Then Nathan said to David, "You are that man!"*

Hold them accountable.

PROMISE FROM GOD: Joshua 1:9 *Be strong and courageous! . . . For the LORD your God is with you wherever you go.*

LISTENING

Does God really listen when I pray?

Psalm 17:6 *I am praying to you because I know you will answer, O God. Bend down and listen as I pray.*

Psalm 102:17 *He will listen to the prayers of the destitute. He will not reject their pleas.*

Psalm 116:2 *Because he bends down and listens, I will pray as long as I have breath!*

LISTENING

Isaiah 59:1 *Listen! The LORD is not too weak to save you, and he is not becoming deaf. He can hear you when you call.*

1 John 5:14-15 *We can be confident that he will listen to us whenever we ask him for anything in line with his will. And if we know he is listening when we make our requests, we can be sure that he will give us what we ask for.*

God hears every prayer, listens carefully, and he does answer. His answer may be "yes," "no," or "wait, not now."

How can I improve my listening to God?

Psalm 5:3 *Listen to my voice in the morning, LORD. Each morning I bring my requests to you and wait expectantly.*

I should come to God regularly and wait expectantly.

Psalm 46:10 *Be silent, and know that I am God!*

I should find times to be quiet and meditate.

Luke 8:18 *Be sure to pay attention to what you hear. To those who are open to my teaching, more understanding will be given. But to those who are not listening, even what they think they have will be taken away from them.*

Hebrews 2:1 *We must listen very carefully to the truth we have heard, or we may drift away from it.*

I should be attentive to God's Word.

1 Kings 19:12 *After the earthquake there was a fire, but the LORD was not in the fire. And after the fire there was the sound of a gentle whisper.*

I should recognize that God sometimes speaks to us in quietness.

John 10:27 *My sheep recognize my voice; I know them, and they follow me.*

I should recognize the Shepherd's voice and follow him.

In addition to God, to whom should I listen?

Proverbs 10:20 *The words of the godly are like sterling silver; the heart of a fool is worthless.*

I should listen to godly people.

1 Kings 10:24 *People from every nation came to visit him and to hear the wisdom God had given him.*

I should listen to those filled with God's wisdom.

1 Samuel 3:19 *As Samuel grew up, the LORD was with him, and everything Samuel said was wise and helpful.*

I should listen to those who walk with God.

1 Chronicles 13:1 *David consulted with all his officials, including the generals and captains of his army.*

I should listen to wise and skilled leaders.

Proverbs 1:7-9 *Fear of the LORD is the beginning of knowledge. Only fools despise wisdom and discipline. Listen, my child, to what your father teaches you. Don't neglect your mother's teaching. What you learn from them will crown you with grace and clothe you with honor.*

Children should listen to their parents.

Proverbs 5:13 *Oh, why didn't I listen to my teachers? Why didn't I pay attention to those who gave me instruction?*

Students should listen to their teachers.

PROMISE FROM GOD: Proverbs 1:23 *Come here and listen to me! I'll pour out the spirit of wisdom upon you and make you wise.*

LONELINESS

Why does God allow us to get lonely?

Genesis 2:18 *The LORD God said, "It is not good for the man to be alone. I will make a companion who will help him."*

God did not intend for us to be lonely. Quite the contrary, it was God who recognized Adam's need for companionship. He gave Adam the task of naming the animals so that Adam could recognize his own need for a companion. It was then that God created woman.

Romans 8:38-39 *I am convinced that nothing can ever separate us from his love. Death can't, and life can't. The angels can't, and the demons can't. Our fears for today, our worries about tomorrow, and even the powers of hell can't keep God's love away. Whether we are high above the sky or in the deepest ocean, nothing in all creation will ever be able to separate us from the love of God that is revealed in Christ Jesus our Lord.*

God never intended for us to be alone. He has promised us that he will always be there. Nothing can separate us from him. He intended for us to have human relationships as well as a spiritual one.

How can I avoid loneliness?

Romans 12:5 *Since we are all one body in Christ, we belong to each other, and each of us needs all the others.*

Hebrews 10:25 *Let us not neglect our meeting together, as some people do, but encourage and warn each other, especially now that the day of his coming back again is drawing near.*

The best way to avoid loneliness is to get together with other believers. Get involved in a local church.

≣PROMISE FROM GOD: Psalm 23:4 *Even when I walk through the dark valley of death I will not be afraid, for you are close beside me.*

*L*OSS

See GRIEF AND LOSS

*L*OVE

Must I love other people? What if I don't want to?

John 13:34-35 *Now I am giving you a new commandment: Love each other. Just as I have loved you, you should love each other. Your love for one another will prove to the world that you are my disciples.*

1 Peter 4:8 *Love covers a multitude of sins.*

1 John 2:9 *If anyone says, "I am living in the light" but hates a Christian brother or sister, that person is still living in darkness.*

1 John 4:12 *If we love each other, God lives in us, and his love has been brought to full expression through us.*

Being a Christian comes with certain expectations, and one of them is that we will love others. Our Christian conduct is proof of whether we love each other, and loving each other is proof that we belong to Christ.

What are some special things that come from a loving relationship?

Proverbs 10:12 *Hatred stirs up quarrels, but love covers all offenses.*

1 Corinthians 13:4-7 *Love is patient and kind. Love is not jealous or boastful or proud or rude. Love does not demand its own way. Love is not irritable, and it keeps no record of when it has been wronged. It is never glad about injustice but rejoices whenever the truth wins out. Love never gives up, never loses faith, is always hopeful, and endures through every circumstance.*

The gifts that come from love are many. Here are a few: 1) forgiveness, 2) patience, 3) kindness, 4) love for truth, 5) love for justice, 6) love for the best in a person, 7) loyalty at any cost, 8) belief in a person no matter what. Love does not allow for 1) jealousy, 2) envy, 3) pride, 4) a haughty spirit, 5) selfishness, 6) rudeness, 7) a demand for one's own way, 8) irritability, 9) grudges.

Does God really love me? How can I know?

Hosea 2:19 *I will make you my wife forever, showing you righteousness and justice, unfailing love and compassion.*

John 3:16 *God so loved the world that he gave his only Son, so that everyone who believes in him will not perish but have eternal life.*

Romans 5:5 *[God] has given us the Holy Spirit to fill our hearts with his love.*

Romans 8:38 *Nothing can ever separate us from his love.*

1 John 4:9-10 *God showed how much he loved us by sending his only Son into the world so that we might have eternal life through him. This is real love.*

How should we show our love to God?

Matthew 10:42 *If you give even a cup of cold water to one of the least of my followers, you will surely be rewarded.*
By showing our love to needy people whom God loves

John 14:21 *Those who obey my commandments are the ones who love me.*
By obeying him

John 21:15-17 *Do you love me? . . . Feed my lambs. . . . Take care of my sheep. . . . Feed my sheep.*

Hebrews 6:10 *He will not forget . . . how you have shown your love to him by caring for other Christians.*
By guiding and helping Jesus' followers

Psalm 122:1 *I was glad when they said to me, "Let us go to the house of the LORD."*
By worshiping him and praising him for his love to us

PROMISE FROM GOD: Romans 8:39 *Whether we are high above the sky or in the deepest ocean, nothing in all creation will ever be able to separate us from the love of God that is revealed in Christ Jesus our Lord.*

MARRIAGE

What kind of relationship should a marriage be?

Genesis 2:18 *The LORD God said, "It is not good for the man to be alone. I will make a companion who will help him."*

Ecclesiastes 4:9-10 *Two people can accomplish more than twice as much as one. . . . If one person falls, the other can reach out and help.*

Matthew 19:4-6 *"Haven't you read the Scriptures?" Jesus replied. "They record that from the beginning 'God made them male and female.' And he said, 'This explains why a man leaves his father and mother and is joined to his wife, and the two are united into one.' Since they are no longer two but one, let no one separate them, for God has joined them together."*

1 Corinthians 11:3 *There is one thing I want you to know: A man is responsible to Christ, a woman is responsible to her husband, and Christ is responsible to God.*

Marriage at its best is a relationship so close and intimate that the two of you work together as one. It involves mutual trust, mutual support, mutual defense, mutual comfort, mutual vulnerability, mutual responsibility.

How should a husband treat his wife?

Proverbs 18:22 *The man who finds a wife finds a treasure and receives favor from the LORD.*

Ecclesiastes 9:9 *Live happily with the woman you love through all the meaningless days of life that God has given you in this world. The wife God gives you is your reward for all your earthly toil.*

Ephesians 5:21 *And further, you will submit to one another out of reverence for Christ.*

1 Peter 3:7 *In the same way, you husbands must give honor to your wives. Treat her with understanding as you live together. She may be weaker than you are, but she is your* *equal partner in God's gift of new life. If you don't treat her as you should, your prayers will not be heard.*

Husbands should love their wives sacrificially, with the depth of love that Christ showed when he died for us.

How should a wife treat her husband?

Proverbs 31:11-12 *Her husband can trust her, and she will greatly enrich his life. She will not hinder him but help him all her life.*

Ephesians 5:22-24 *You wives will submit to your husbands as you do to the Lord. For a husband is the head of his wife as Christ is the head of his body, the church; he gave his life to be her Savior. As the church submits to Christ, so you wives must submit to your husbands in everything.*

A wife should love her husband sacrificially, helping and supporting him, believing in him, and submitting to him.

What is the importance of loyalty in a marriage?

Malachi 2:15 *Didn't the LORD make you one with your wife? In body and spirit you are his. And what does he want? Godly children from your union. So guard yourself; remain loyal to the wife of your youth.*

God commands husbands and wives to be loyal to one another. He does not merely suggest this.

Proverbs 5:15, 18-19 *Drink water from your own well—share your love only with your wife. . . . Let your wife be a fountain of blessing for you. Rejoice in the wife of your youth. She is a loving doe, a graceful deer. Let her breasts satisfy you always. May you always be captivated by her love.*

1 Corinthians 7:3-4 *The husband should not deprive his wife of sexual intimacy, which is her right as a married*

woman, nor should the wife deprive her husband. The wife gives authority over her body to her husband, and the husband also gives authority over his body to his wife.

Hebrews 13:4 *Give honor to marriage, and remain faithful to one another in marriage. God will surely judge people who are immoral and those who commit adultery.*

Husbands and wives must be faithful to each other, seeking to satisfy and honor each other.

If a person's mate dies, is it all right to marry again?

1 Corinthians 7:39 *A wife is married to her husband as long as he lives. If her husband dies, she is free to marry whomever she wishes, but this must be a marriage acceptable to the Lord.*

Marriage is a lifetime commitment. When a mate dies, the marriage contract is over. It is not wrong for the survivor to marry again.

PROMISE FROM GOD: Ephesians 5:31 *As the Scriptures say, "A man leaves his father and mother and is joined to his wife, and the two are united into one."*

MEDITATION

To whom should my meditation be directed?

Psalm 63:6 *I lie awake thinking of you, meditating on you through the night.*

My moments of meditation are about God and to God.

How do I meditate? What is involved in meditation?

Psalm 62:1, 5 *I wait quietly before God, for my salvation comes from him. . . . I wait quietly before God, for my hope is in him.*

Meditation is waiting quietly and patiently before God, putting my hope in him.

Psalm 1:2 *They delight in doing everything the LORD wants; day and night they think about his law.*

Meditation is thinking about God's Word and what God tells us through his Word.

Psalm 16:7 *I will bless the LORD who guides me; even at night my heart instructs me.*

Meditation is a time of seeking God's guidance and instruction.

Psalm 143:5 *I remember the days of old. I ponder all your great works. I think about what you have done.*

Meditation is a time of reflection on God's past blessings.

What should I think about when I meditate?

Psalm 48:9 *O God, we meditate on your unfailing love as we worship in your Temple.*

I should think about God's unfailing love.

Psalm 77:11-12 *I recall all you have done, O LORD; I remember your wonderful deeds of long ago. They are constantly in my thoughts. I cannot stop thinking about them.*

I should think about all God has done for me.

Psalm 145:5 *I will meditate on your majestic, glorious splendor and your wonderful miracles.*

I should think about God's majestic, glorious splendor.

Romans 8:5 *Those who are dominated by the sinful nature think about sinful things, but those who are controlled by the Holy Spirit think about things that please the Spirit.*
I should think about the Holy Spirit and what pleases him.

Philippians 4:8 *And now, dear brothers and sisters, let me say one more thing as I close this letter. Fix your thoughts on what is true and honorable and right. Think about things that are pure and lovely and admirable. Think about things that are excellent and worthy of praise.*
I should think about things that are true, honorable, right, pure, lovely, admirable, excellent, and worthy of praise.

Psalm 119:97 *Oh, how I love your law! I think about it all day long.*
I should think about God's Word.

PROMISE FROM GOD: 2 Timothy 2:7 *Think about what I am saying. The Lord will give you understanding in all these things.*

MEMORIES

What do I do with bad memories?

Genesis 41:51 *Joseph named his older son Manasseh, for he said, "God has made me forget all my troubles and the family of my father."*

Isaiah 54:4 *Fear not; you will no longer live in shame. The shame of your youth and the sorrows of widowhood will be remembered no more.*

Philippians 3:13 *No, dear brothers and sisters, I am still not all I should be, but I am focusing all my energies on this one thing: Forgetting the past and looking forward to what lies ahead.*

God, who forgives, can also help us forget bad memories.

What place does God desire to have in my memory?

Exodus 31:13 *Tell the people of Israel to keep my Sabbath day, for the Sabbath is a sign of the covenant between me and you forever. It helps you to remember that I am the LORD, who makes you holy.*

Deuteronomy 4:9 *Watch out! Be very careful never to forget what you have seen the LORD do for you. Do not let these things escape from your mind as long as you live! And be sure to pass them on to your children and grandchildren.*

Psalm 103:2 *Praise the LORD, I tell myself, and never forget the good things he does for me.*

Psalm 111:4 *Who can forget the wonders he performs? How gracious and merciful is our LORD!*

Psalm 119:16, 93 *I will delight in your principles and not forget your word. . . . I will never forget your commandments, for you have used them to restore my joy and health.*

2 Timothy 2:8 *Never forget that Jesus Christ was a man born into King David's family and that he was raised from the dead. This is the Good News I preach.*

Hebrews 10:32 *Don't ever forget those early days when you first learned about Christ. Remember how you remained faithful even though it meant terrible suffering.*

We must never forget the Lord and what he has done for us.

What is the danger of forgetting God?

1 Samuel 12:9 *The people soon forgot about the LORD their God, so he let them be conquered by Sisera, the general of Hazor's army, and by the Philistines and the king of Moab.*

Job 8:13-14 *Such is the fate of all who forget God. The hope of the godless comes to nothing. Everything they count on will collapse. They are leaning on a spiderweb.*

Jeremiah 3:21 *Voices are heard high on the windswept mountains, the weeping and pleading of Israel's people. For they have forgotten the LORD their God and wandered far from his ways.*

Ezekiel 23:35 *Because you have forgotten me and turned your back on me, says the Sovereign LORD, you must bear the consequences of all your lewdness and prostitution.*

When we forget God, we have nothing left but sin and self, and what will those do for our eternal future? Forgetting God leaves us to the consequences of sin without the benefits of God's gracious mercy.

PROMISE FROM GOD: Psalm 112:6 *Those who are righteous will be long remembered.*

ERCY

What is mercy?

Psalm 103:8-10 *The LORD is merciful and gracious; he is slow to get angry and full of unfailing love. He will not constantly accuse us, nor remain angry forever. He has not punished us for all our sins, nor does he deal with us as we deserve.*

Isaiah 63:9 *In all their suffering he also suffered, and he personally rescued them. In his love and mercy he redeemed them. He lifted them up and carried them through all the years.*

Lamentations 3:22 *The unfailing love of the LORD never ends! By his mercies we have been kept from complete destruction.*

Micah 7:18 *Where is another God like you, who pardons the sins of the survivors among his people? You cannot stay angry with your people forever, because you delight in showing mercy.*

1 Peter 1:3 *All honor to the God and Father of our Lord Jesus Christ, for it is by his boundless mercy that God has given us the privilege of being born again.*
Mercy is not receiving the punishment we should receive for our sins. By his mercy God forgives our sins and opens up eternal life to us.

Who receives mercy?

Psalm 119:132 *Come and show me your mercy, as you do for all who love your name.*

Matthew 5:7 *God blesses those who are merciful, for they will be shown mercy.*

Luke 1:50 *His mercy goes on from generation to generation, to all who fear him.*
God promises his mercy to those who love him, fear (revere) him, and show mercy to others.

Romans 9:15-16 *God said to Moses, "I will show mercy to anyone I choose, and I will show compassion to anyone I choose." So receiving God's promise is not up to us. We can't get it by choosing it or working hard for it. God will show mercy to anyone he chooses.*

Ultimately, God chooses who will receive his mercy. We cannot earn it. We are, literally, at his mercy.

How can I show mercy?

Colossians 3:12-13 *Since God chose you to be the holy people whom he loves, you must clothe yourselves with tender-hearted mercy, kindness, humility, gentleness, and patience. You must make allowance for each other's faults and forgive the person who offends you. Remember, the Lord forgave you, so you must forgive others.*

I can forgive others.

Matthew 18:33 *Shouldn't you have mercy on your fellow servant, just as I had mercy on you?*

I can share the mercy God has given me.

Micah 6:8 *No, O people, the LORD has already told you what is good, and this is what he requires: to do what is right, to love mercy, and to walk humbly with your God.*

I can show mercy as an act of obedience to God.

Zechariah 7:9 *This is what the LORD Almighty says: Judge fairly and honestly, and show mercy and kindness to one another.*

I can show mercy in judging fairly and honestly and in showing kindness to others.

James 3:17 *The wisdom that comes from heaven is first of all pure. It is also peace loving, gentle at all times, and willing to yield to others. It is full of mercy and good deeds. It shows no partiality and is always sincere.*

When I have God's wisdom, I will know how to show mercy.

PROMISE FROM GOD: Psalm 103:8 *The LORD is merciful and gracious; he is slow to get angry and full of unfailing love.*

MISTAKES

What does the Bible have to say about mistakes?

Genesis 3:12-13 *"Yes," Adam admitted, "but it was the woman you gave me who brought me the fruit." . . . "The serpent tricked me," she replied.*

Both Adam and Eve responded to mistakes by shifting the blame.

Judges 16:17, 21, 28 *Finally, Samson told her his secret. . . . so the Philistines captured him and gouged out his eyes. . . . Then Samson prayed to the LORD, "Sovereign Lord, remember me again."*

Samson's life, although filled with foolish mistakes, was still mightily used by God.

James 3:2 *We all make many mistakes, but those who control their tongues can also control themselves in every other way.*

One of the most common mistakes is saying something we later regret.

Jonah 1:3 *But Jonah got up and went in the opposite direction in order to get away from the LORD.*

The worst mistake we can make is running from God.

Exodus 2:12 *After looking around to make sure no one was watching, Moses killed the Egyptian and buried him in the sand.*

Even Moses' life was marred by an immature and terrible mistake.

Matthew 26:74 *Peter said, "I swear by God, I don't know the man."*

Christ restored Peter to fellowship even after Peter's most painful mistake.

PROMISE FROM GOD: Philippians 3:13
No, dear brothers and sisters, I am still not all I should be, but I am focusing all my energies on this one thing: Forgetting the past and looking forward to what lies ahead.

*M*ONEY

What is a proper perspective toward money?

Psalm 23:1 *The LORD is my shepherd; I have everything I need.*

Matthew 6:24 *No one can serve two masters. . . . You cannot serve both God and money.*

The love of money can get our priorities out of line. We must keep reminding ourselves that God must be first in our lives and that money cannot satisfy our deepest needs.

Psalm 119:36 *Give me an eagerness for your decrees; do not inflict me with love for money!*

1 Timothy 6:10 *The love of money is at the root of all kinds of evil.*

Hebrews 13:5 *Stay away from the love of money; be satisfied with what you have. For God has said, "I will never fail you. I will never forsake you."*

Money is not the root of all evil; the love of it is!

Proverbs 11:28 *Trust in your money and down you go!*

Isaiah 55:2 *Why spend your money on food that does not give you strength? . . . Listen, and I will tell you where to get food that is good for the soul!*

Too often we buy things to fill a void or an emotional need in our lives. The Bible points to a way to acquire a deep and lasting happiness that always satisfies.

Proverbs 19:1 *It is better to be poor and honest than to be a fool and dishonest.*

Mark 8:36 *How do you benefit if you gain the whole world but lose your own soul in the process?*

No amount of money is worth it if it was gained deceptively or dishonestly. Taking advantage of others to make money is stealing. Those who do this lose far more than they could ever gain.

Philippians 4:11-12 *I have learned how to get along happily whether I have much or little. . . . I have learned the secret of living in every situation.*

Philippians 4:19 *This same God who takes care of me will supply all your needs from his glorious riches.*

The Bible promises that God will supply all of our needs. The problem comes when our definition of "need" is different from God's. The first thing we must do is study God's Word to discover what he says we need for a fulfilling life.

Mark 12:43 *He called his disciples to him and said, "I assure you, this poor widow has given more than all the others have given."*

1 John 3:17 *If one of you has money enough to live well and sees a brother or sister in need and refuses to help—how can God's love be in that person?*

Consistently and generously giving away our money might be the most effective way to keep us from loving it. When we see what giving does in the lives of others, needs are met in us that material possessions could never satisfy. This kind of giving measures our Christian love.

Proverbs 3:9-10 *Honor the LORD with your wealth and with the best part of everything your land produces. Then he will fill your barns with grain.*

Proverbs 21:20 *Fools spend whatever they get.*

Proverbs 28:19 *Hard workers have plenty of food.*

Malachi 3:10 *"Bring all the tithes into the storehouse. . . . If you do," says the LORD Almighty, "I will open the windows of heaven for you."*

Matthew 25:14 *He called together his servants and gave them money to invest for him while he was gone.*

Luke 6:38 *If you give, you will receive.*

1 Corinthians 4:12 *We have worked wearily with our own hands to earn our living.*

2 Corinthians 9:6 *The one who plants generously will get a generous crop.*

1 Thessalonians 4:12 *You will not need to depend on others to meet your financial needs.*

God urges us to be good stewards in earning, spending, and saving our money. He understands the importance of providing for the needs of our family and the future. But he also expects us to use our money generously to help others.

Why don't I ever seem to have enough?

Isaiah 55:2 *Why spend your money on food that does not give you strength?*
Because we foolishly spend our money on what does not satisfy the soul

Haggai 1:4 *Why are you living in luxurious houses while my house lies in ruins?*
Because we don't manage our money according to God's priorities

Luke 12:15 *Don't be greedy for what you don't have. Real life is not measured by how much we own.*
Because we depend on our wealth to bring security

PROMISE FROM GOD: Matthew 6:31-33
Don't worry about having enough food or drink or clothing. Why be like the pagans who are so deeply concerned about these things? Your heavenly Father already knows all your needs, and he will give you all you need from day to day if you live for him and make the Kingdom of God your primary concern.

OTHERS

What qualities should a mother possess?

1 Kings 3:26-27 *Then the woman who really was the mother of the living child, and who loved him very much, cried out, "Oh no, my lord! Give her the child—please do not kill him!" But the other woman said, "All right, he will be neither yours nor mine; divide him between us!" Then the king said, "Do not kill him, but give the baby to the woman who wants him to live, for she is his mother!"*

A wise mother should love her children unselfishly, wanting what is best for the child above what is best for herself.

1 Thessalonians 2:7 *As apostles of Christ we certainly had a right to make some demands of you, but we were as gentle among you as a mother feeding and caring for her own children.*

A wise mother is gentle with her children.

Hebrews 11:23 *It was by faith that Moses' parents hid him for three months. They saw that God had given them an unusual child, and they were not afraid of what the king might do.*

A wise mother exercises great faith for her children.

Proverbs 14:1 *A wise woman builds her house; a foolish woman tears hers down with her own hands.*

A wise mother builds her family up rather than tearing them down with hurtful words.

What are some of the responsibilities of a mother?

Proverbs 4:3 *I, too, was once my father's son, tenderly loved by my mother as an only child.*
A mother should love her children.

Luke 18:15 *One day some parents brought their little children to Jesus so he could touch them and bless them.*
A mother should lead her children to Jesus.

2 Timothy 1:5 *I know that you sincerely trust the Lord, for you have the faith of your mother, Eunice, and your grandmother, Lois.*
A mother should be a woman with great faith in God, which can become a great heritage for her family.

Deuteronomy 8:5 *You should realize that just as a parent disciplines a child, the LORD your God disciplines you to help you.*
A wise mother disciplines her children with the same loving hand the Lord shows to her.

Proverbs 1:8 *Listen, my child, to what your father teaches you. Don't neglect your mother's teaching.*
A mother teaches her children God's way.

Isaiah 66:12-13 *"Peace and prosperity will overflow Jerusalem like a river," says the LORD. "The wealth of the nations will flow to her. Her children will be nursed at her breasts, carried in her arms, and treated with love. I will comfort you there as a child is comforted by its mother."*
A mother comforts her children.

Mark 10:7 *This explains why a man leaves his father and mother and is joined to his wife.*

A mother raises her children to become mature and independent young people.

What does the Bible say about the role of parents?

2 Timothy 3:15 *You have been taught the holy Scriptures from childhood.*

Parents are to take responsibility for teaching their children a love for the Word of God.

Proverbs 3:12 *The LORD corrects those he loves, just as a father corrects a child in whom he delights.*

Hebrews 12:11 *No discipline is enjoyable while it is happening—it is painful! But afterward there will be a quiet harvest of right living.*

Parents are to discipline their children with consistency, wisdom, and love.

Genesis 25:28 *Isaac loved Esau . . . but Rebekah favored Jacob.*

Parents are not to show favoritism between children.

1 Samuel 2:29 *Why do you honor your sons more than me?*

Parents who are too indulgent do not help their children develop character.

Luke 15:20 *Filled with love and compassion, he ran to his son, embraced him, and kissed him.*

The mark of a loving parent is the willingness to forgive.

PROMISE FROM GOD: Exodus 20:12 *Honor your father and mother. Then you will live a long, full life in the land the LORD your God will give you.*

MOURNING

See GRIEF and LOSS

MOVING

How can I best handle (another) move?

Joshua 1:9 *I command you—be strong and courageous! Do not be afraid or discouraged. For the LORD your God is with you wherever you go.*

Psalm 139:3-10 *You chart the path ahead of me and tell me where to stop and rest. Every moment you know where I am. . . . You both precede and follow me. You place your hand of blessing on my head. . . . I can never escape from your spirit! I can never get away from your presence! . . . If I dwell by the farthest oceans, even there your hand will guide me, and your strength will support me.*

When I move to a new place, I should recognize that God is already there, preparing that place for me and me for that place.

Numbers 9:21 *Sometimes the cloud stayed only overnight and moved on the next morning. But day or night, when the cloud lifted, the people broke camp and followed.*

When I move to a new place, I must pray for the Lord's presence to be with me at all times.

Numbers 10:13 *When the time to move arrived, the LORD gave the order through Moses.*

I should seek the Lord's direction in each move I make.

Genesis 13:18 *Then Abram moved his camp to the oak grove owned by Mamre, which is at Hebron. There he built an altar to the LORD.*

Throughout any move I make I must continue to worship the Lord regularly.

How can God help me in my move?

Exodus 33:14-15 *The LORD replied, "I will personally go with you, Moses. I will give you rest—everything will be fine for you." Then Moses said, "If you don't go with us personally, don't let us move a step from this place."*

2 Samuel 2:1 *David asked the LORD, "Should I move back to Judah?" And the LORD replied, "Yes." Then David asked, "Which town should I go to?" And the LORD replied, "Hebron."*

Ezra 8:21 *There by the Ahava Canal, I gave orders for all of us to fast and humble ourselves before our God. We prayed that he would give us a safe journey and protect us, our children, and our goods as we traveled.*

Isaiah 41:13 *I am holding you by your right hand—I, the LORD your God. And I say to you, "Do not be afraid. I am here to help you."*

God will guide us, give us wisdom and courage, and be with us wherever our move takes us—if only we ask him.

PROMISE FROM GOD: Joshua 1:9 *The LORD your God is with you wherever you go.*

EEDS

What do I really need?

Matthew 5:3 *God blesses those who realize their need for him, for the Kingdom of Heaven is given to them.*
I need God—his love, his presence, his promise of eternal life.

Acts 13:24 *Before [Jesus] came, John the Baptist preached the need for everyone in Israel to turn from sin and turn to God and be baptized.*
I need to repent of my sins and turn to God.

Hebrews 7:26 *He is the kind of high priest we need because he is holy and blameless, unstained by sin. He has now been set apart from sinners, and he has been given the highest place of honor in heaven.*
I need Jesus—his mercy, his salvation, and his forgiveness.

Luke 17:5 *One day the apostles said to the Lord, "We need more faith; tell us how to get it."*

Ephesians 6:16 *In every battle you will need faith as your shield to stop the fiery arrows aimed at you by Satan.*
I need more faith.

Psalm 119:19 *I am but a foreigner here on earth; I need the guidance of your commands. Don't hide them from me!*
I need God's guidance.

James 1:5 *If you need wisdom—if you want to know what God wants you to do—ask him, and he will gladly tell you. He will not resent your asking.*
I need God's wisdom.

NEEDS

Colossians 1:11 *We also pray that you will be strength-*
ened with his glorious power so that you will have all the
patience and endurance you need. May you be filled with joy.

Hebrews 10:36 *Patient endurance is what you need now,*
so you will continue to do God's will. Then you will receive
all that he has promised.

I need patient endurance to continue to do God's will.

2 Corinthians 12:9 *Each time he said, "My gracious*
favor is all you need. My power works best in your weakness."
So now I am glad to boast about my weaknesses, so that the
power of Christ may work through me.

Hebrews 4:16 *Let us come boldly to the throne of our*
gracious God. There we will receive his mercy, and we will
find grace to help us when we need it.

I need God's mercy and grace in times of weakness or
when I fail him.

Psalm 138:3 *When I pray, you answer me; you encourage*
me by giving me the strength I need.

Philippians 4:13 *For I can do everything with the help*
of Christ who gives me the strength I need.

I need God's strength to do what I can't do on my own.

Luke 18:1 *One day Jesus told his disciples a story to*
illustrate their need for constant prayer and to show them that
they must never give up.

I need prayer to keep me in constant communication with
God.

Psalm 119:75 *I know, O LORD, that your decisions are*
fair; you disciplined me because I needed it.

I need the Lord's discipline to keep me following his ways.

Romans 12:5 *So it is with Christ's body. We are all parts of his one body, and each of us has different work to do. And since we are all one body in Christ, we belong to each other, and each of us needs all the others.*

I need other Christians, encouraging me and serving with me.

Psalm 145:15 *All eyes look to you for help; you give them their food as they need it.*

I need food and other provisions of life.

On whom should I depend to meet my needs?

Matthew 6:33 *He will give you all you need from day to day if you live for him and make the Kingdom of God your primary concern.*

Romans 5:6 *When we were utterly helpless, Christ came at just the right time and died for us sinners.*

2 Corinthians 9:8 *God will generously provide all you need. Then you will always have everything you need and plenty left over to share with others.*

2 Peter 1:3 *As we know Jesus better, his divine power gives us everything we need for living a godly life. He has called us to receive his own glory and goodness!*

Having an eternal perspective shows you that what you really need is what God supplies in great abundance.

PROMISE FROM GOD: Philippians 4:19 *This same God who takes care of me will supply all your needs from his glorious riches, which have been given to us in Christ Jesus.*

$\mathcal{N}$ EIGHBORS

Who is my neighbor?

Luke 10:29-37 *The man wanted to justify his actions, so he asked Jesus, "And who is my neighbor?" Jesus replied with an illustration: "A Jewish man was traveling on a trip from Jerusalem to Jericho, and he was attacked by bandits. They stripped him of his clothes and money, beat him up, and left him half dead beside the road. . . . A Jewish priest came along . . . and passed him by. A Temple assistant walked over . . . but he also passed by on the other side. Then a despised Samaritan came along, and when he saw the man, he felt deep pity. . . . He took care of him. . . . Now which of these three would you say was a neighbor to the man who was attacked by bandits?" Jesus asked. The man replied, "The one who showed him mercy." Then Jesus said, "Yes, now go and do the same."*

Your neighbor is anyone who needs God's mercy, forgiveness, compassion, and friendship.

What are my responsibilities to my neighbor?

Leviticus 19:18 *Never seek revenge or bear a grudge against anyone, but love your neighbor as yourself. I am the LORD.*

Deuteronomy 22:1-4 *If you see your neighbor's ox or sheep wandering away, don't pretend not to see it. Take it back to its owner. . . . Do the same if you find your neighbor's donkey, clothing, or anything else your neighbor loses. Don't pretend you did not see it. If you see your neighbor's ox or donkey lying on the road, do not look the other way. Go and help your neighbor get it to its feet!*

Proverbs 3:28 *If you can help your neighbor now, don't say, "Come back tomorrow, and then I'll help you."*

Romans 13:9-10 *The commandments against adultery and murder and stealing and coveting—and any other commandment—are all summed up in this one commandment: "Love your neighbor as yourself." Love does no wrong to anyone, so love satisfies all of God's requirements.*

James 2:8 *Yes indeed, it is good when you truly obey our Lord's royal command found in the Scriptures: "Love your neighbor as yourself."*

When we love our neighbor, we will help our neighbor in times of need.

Leviticus 19:15-17 *Always judge your neighbors fairly, neither favoring the poor nor showing deference to the rich. Do not spread slanderous gossip among your people. Do not try to get ahead at the cost of your neighbor's life, for I am the LORD. . . . Confront your neighbors directly so you will not be held guilty for their crimes.*

Ephesians 4:25 *Put away all falsehood and "tell your neighbor the truth" because we belong to each other.*

When we love our neighbor, we will tell the truth, even when it is painful.

Exodus 20:16 *Do not testify falsely against your neighbor.*

When we love our neighbor, we will not tell lies about him or her.

Proverbs 3:29 *Do not plot against your neighbors, for they trust you.*

When we love our neighbors, we will not break their trust by plotting against them.

NEIGHBORS

Proverbs 11:12 *It is foolish to belittle a neighbor; a person with good sense remains silent.*

When we love our neighbors, we will not make fun of them.

Deuteronomy 5:21 *Do not covet your neighbor's wife. Do not covet your neighbor's house or land, male or female servant, ox or donkey, or anything else your neighbor owns.*

When we love our neighbors, we will not want what they have.

Proverbs 25:17 *Don't visit your neighbors too often, or you will wear out your welcome.*

Proverbs 27:14 *If you shout a pleasant greeting to your neighbor too early in the morning, it will be counted as a curse!*

When we love our neighbors, we will respect their time and privacy.

How should I live among my non-Christian neighbors?

Colossians 4:5-6 *Live wisely among those who are not Christians, and make the most of every opportunity. Let your conversation be gracious and effective so that you will have the right answer for everyone.*

James 4:12 *God alone, who made the law, can rightly judge among us. He alone has the power to save or to destroy. So what right do you have to condemn your neighbor?*

1 Peter 2:12 *Be careful how you live among your unbelieving neighbors. Even if they accuse you of doing wrong, they will see your honorable behavior, and they will believe and give honor to God when he comes to judge the world.*

Galatians 5:14   *For the whole law can be summed up in this one command: "Love your neighbor as yourself."*

We should love our non-Christian neighbors, living honorably and graciously before them, being an example of godliness, sharing God's ways with them, and refusing to condemn them.

PROMISE FROM GOD: James 2:8   *Yes indeed, it is good when you truly obey our Lord's royal command found in the Scriptures: "Love your neighbor as yourself."*

OBEDIENCE

Is obedience to God really necessary since we are saved by faith?

Deuteronomy 10:12-13   *And now, Israel, what does the LORD your God require of you? He requires you to fear him, to live according to his will, to love and worship him with all your heart and soul, and to obey the LORD's commands and laws that I am giving you today for your own good.*

Philippians 2:12   *Dearest friends, you were always so careful to follow my instructions when I was with you. And now that I am away you must be even more careful to put into action God's saving work in your lives, obeying God with deep reverence and fear.*

Obedience is putting into action God's saving work in our lives.

Jeremiah 7:23   *Obey me, and I will be your God, and you will be my people. Only do as I say, and all will be well!*

Obedience to God is an intrinsic element of a covenant relationship with him.

Hebrews 11:8 *It was by faith that Abraham obeyed.*
Obedience is an act of faith.

Romans 1:5 *Through Christ, God has given us the privilege and authority to tell Gentiles everywhere what God has done for them, so that they will believe and obey him, bringing glory to his name.*

Romans 6:17 *Thank God! Once you were slaves of sin, but now you have obeyed with all your heart the new teaching God has given you.*
Putting our trust in God for salvation through Christ is equivalent to obeying his message of good news.

Titus 1:16 *Such people claim they know God, but they deny him by the way they live. They are despicable and disobedient, worthless for doing anything good.*
If we are disobedient to God, our claim that we know him is meaningless.

Leviticus 9:6 *Then Moses told them, "When you have followed these instructions from the LORD, the glorious presence of the LORD will appear to you."*

Acts 5:32 *We are witnesses of these things and so is the Holy Spirit, who is given by God to those who obey him.*
God's presence in our lives comes when we obey him.

In what ways does God want us to obey him?
Genesis 6:22 *So Noah did everything exactly as God had commanded him.*

Deuteronomy 5:32 *You must obey all the commands of the LORD your God, following his instructions in every detail.*
God wants us to do everything he commands us to do.

1 Samuel 15:22 *Samuel replied, "What is more pleasing to the LORD: your burnt offerings and sacrifices or your obedience to his voice? Obedience is far better than sacrifice. Listening to him is much better than offering the fat of rams."*
Obedience to God involves listening to what he says.

Exodus 12:28 *The people of Israel did just as the LORD had commanded through Moses and Aaron.*

Romans 13:1 *Obey the government, for God is the one who put it there. All governments have been placed in power by God.*

Hebrews 13:17 *Obey your spiritual leaders and do what they say.*
God shows us what he wants us to do through human authorities.

Exodus 1:17 *Because the midwives feared God, they refused to obey the king and allowed the boys to live, too.*

Acts 4:19-20 *Peter and John replied, "Do you think God wants us to obey you rather than him? We cannot stop telling about the wonderful things we have seen and heard."*

Acts 5:29 *Peter and the apostles replied, "We must obey God rather than human authority."*
We must obey God over human authorities.

PROMISE FROM GOD: Exodus 19:5 *If you will obey me and keep my covenant, you will be my own special treasure from among all the nations of the earth; for all the earth belongs to me.*

PAIN

See SUFFERING

PARENTING

See MOTHERS and
SINGLE PARENTING

PAST

How can I best benefit from the past?

Deuteronomy 32:7 *Remember the days of long ago; think about the generations past. Ask your father and he will inform you. Inquire of your elders, and they will tell you.*

Psalm 78:4 *We will not hide these truths from our children but will tell the next generation about the glorious deeds of the LORD.*

Isaiah 42:23 *Will not even one of you apply these lessons from the past and see the ruin that awaits you?*

1 Corinthians 10:11 *All these events happened to them as examples for us. They were written down to warn us.*

From the past we learn wise lessons of God at work. We also learn from others—what worked well and what didn't. We learn not to repeat failures and how to build on successes.

How can I most effectively deal with a hurtful past?

Genesis 33:4 *Esau ran to meet him and embraced him affectionately and kissed him. Both of them were in tears.*

Genesis 50:19-20 *Joseph told them, "Don't be afraid of me. Am I God, to judge and punish you? As far as I am concerned, God turned into good what you meant for evil."*

Matthew 5:23-24 *If you are standing before the altar in the Temple, offering a sacrifice to God, and you suddenly remember that someone has something against you, leave your sacrifice there beside the altar. Go and be reconciled to that person. Then come and offer your sacrifice to God.*

Matthew 18:21-22 *Peter came to him and asked, "Lord, how often should I forgive someone who sins against me? Seven times?" "No!" Jesus replied, "seventy times seven!"*

Luke 23:34 *Jesus said, "Father, forgive these people, because they don't know what they are doing." And the soldiers gambled for his clothes by throwing dice.*

The hurts of the past can be forgotten if they are forgiven.

How do I deal with regrets?

Psalm 51:7, 9-10 *Purify me from my sins, and I will be clean; wash me, and I will be whiter than snow. . . . Don't keep looking at my sins. Remove the stain of my guilt. Create in me a clean heart, O God. Renew a right spirit within me.*

Isaiah 1:18 *"Come now, let us argue this out," says the LORD. "No matter how deep the stain of your sins, I can remove it. I can make you as clean as freshly fallen snow. Even if you are stained as red as crimson, I can make you as white as wool."*

Romans 4:6-8 *King David spoke of this, describing the happiness of an undeserving sinner who is declared to be righteous: "Oh, what joy for those whose disobedience is forgiven, whose sins are put out of sight. Yes, what joy for those whose sin is no longer counted against them by the Lord."*

Philippians 3:13 *No, dear brothers and sisters, I am still not all I should be, but I am focusing all my energies on this one thing: Forgetting the past and looking forward to what lies ahead.*

Regrets are like a dirty window that keeps us from seeing clearly what is in front of us. But God is in the cleaning business. He washes away the sins of the past as well as the guilt over those sins. If he forgets them completely, so can you.

PROMISE FROM GOD: Isaiah 1:18 *No matter how deep the stain of your sins, I can remove it. I can make you as clean as freshly fallen snow. Even if you are stained as red as crimson, I can make you as white as wool.*

PATIENCE

How can I grow in patience?

Exodus 5:22-23 *Moses went back to the LORD and protested, . . . "Why did you send me?"*

We become impatient when we focus more on our agenda than on God's will.

Psalm 40:1 *I waited patiently for the LORD to help me, and he turned to me and heard my cry.*

We must wait patiently in prayer for God to do his work in us.

Habakkuk 2:3 *If it seems slow, wait patiently, for it will surely take place. It will not be delayed.*

We develop patience as we learn to live with an eternal perspective.

Galatians 5:22 *When the Holy Spirit controls our lives, he will produce this kind of fruit in us: love, joy, peace, patience.*

Patience is a by-product of the presence and work of the Holy Spirit in our heart.

1 Corinthians 13:4 *Love is patient and kind.*

Patience is one of the evidences of love.

Romans 8:25 *If we look forward to something we don't have yet, we must wait patiently and confidently.*

Patience in difficulty looks forward with hope in God's eternal glory.

PROMISE FROM GOD: Lamentations 3:25 *The LORD is wonderfully good to those who wait for him and seek him.*

PRAISE

Why is it so important to praise God?

1 Chronicles 16:25-26 *Great is the LORD! He is most worthy of praise! He is to be revered above all gods. The gods of other nations are merely idols, but the LORD made the heavens!*

PRAISE

Psalm 89:5 *All heaven will praise your miracles, LORD; myriads of angels will praise you for your faithfulness.*

Psalm 92:1 *It is good to give thanks to the LORD, to sing praises to the Most High.*

Psalm 106:2 *Who can list the glorious miracles of the LORD? Who can ever praise him half enough?*

Luke 19:36-37 *The crowds spread out their coats on the road ahead of Jesus. As they reached the place where the road started down from the Mount of Olives, all of his followers began to shout and sing as they walked along, praising God for all the wonderful miracles they had seen.*

Acts 16:22-25 *A mob quickly formed against Paul and Silas, and the city officials ordered them stripped and beaten with wooden rods. They were severely beaten, and then they were thrown into prison. . . . Around midnight, Paul and Silas were praying and singing hymns to God, and the other prisoners were listening.*

Consider how great God is—the awesome Creator of the universe. Consider how sinful and mortal we are. Then consider how great is God's love for us. How can we help but praise him?

How can I express my praise to God?

Psalm 35:10 *I will praise him from the bottom of my heart.*

Psalm 86:12 *With all my heart I will praise you, O Lord my God. I will give glory to your name forever.*
With all my heart

1 Chronicles 23:30 *Each morning and evening they stood before the LORD to sing songs of thanks and praise to him.*

Psalm 104:33 *I will sing to the LORD as long as I live. I will praise my God to my last breath!*

With all my time

Romans 15:6 *All of you can join together with one voice, giving praise and glory to God, the Father of our Lord Jesus Christ.*

With others

2 Chronicles 20:19 *The Levites from the clans of Kohath and Korah stood to praise the LORD, the God of Israel, with a very loud shout.*

Psalm 34:1 *I will praise the LORD at all times. I will constantly speak his praises.*

With my mouth

1 Chronicles 16:42 *They used their trumpets, cymbals, and other instruments to accompany the songs of praise to God. And the sons of Jeduthun were appointed as gatekeepers.*

Psalm 33:3 *Sing new songs of praise to him; play skillfully on the harp and sing with joy.*

Psalm 47:6-7 *Sing praise to God, sing praises; sing praise to our King, sing praises! For God is the King over all the earth. Praise him with a psalm!*

Psalm 149:1 *Praise the LORD! Sing to the LORD a new song. Sing his praises in the assembly of the faithful.*

Psalm 150:3-5 *Praise him with a blast of the trumpet; praise him with the lyre and harp! Praise him with the tambourine and dancing; praise him with stringed instruments and flutes! Praise him with a clash of cymbals; praise him with loud clanging cymbals.*

With music

Psalm 54:6 *I will sacrifice a voluntary offering to you;
I will praise your name, O LORD, for it is good.*
With an offering

What is the importance of praising others?

Proverbs 27:2 *Don't praise yourself; let others do it!*

Proverbs 31:28 *Her children stand and bless her. Her
husband praises her.*

Proverbs 31:31 *Reward her for all she has done. Let her
deeds publicly declare her praise.*

Matthew 3:16-17 *After his baptism, as Jesus came up
out of the water, the heavens were opened and he saw the
Spirit of God descending like a dove and settling on him.
And a voice from heaven said, "This is my beloved Son,
and I am fully pleased with him."*

Matthew 25:21 *The master was full of praise. "Well
done, my good and faithful servant. You have been faithful
in handling this small amount, so now I will give you many
more responsibilities. Let's celebrate together!"*

We each need to know that others are for us and with us.
Affirmation gives us a sense of worth, encouraging us to
go on.

PROMISE FROM GOD: Psalm 31:21 *Praise the
LORD, for he has shown me his unfailing love.*

PRAYER

What is prayer?

2 Chronicles 7:14 *If my people who are called by my name will humble themselves and pray and seek my face and turn from their wicked ways, I will hear from heaven.*

Prayer is an act of humble worship in which we seek God with all our heart.

Psalm 38:18 *I confess my sins; I am deeply sorry for what I have done.*

1 John 1:9 *If we confess our sins to him, he is faithful and just to forgive us and to cleanse us from every wrong.*

Prayer often begins with a confession of sin.

1 Samuel 14:36 *The priest said, "Let's ask God first."*

2 Samuel 5:19 *David asked the LORD, "Should I go out to fight the Philistines?"*

Prayer is asking God for guidance and waiting for his direction and leading.

Mark 1:35 *The next morning Jesus awoke long before daybreak and went out alone into the wilderness to pray.*

Prayer is an expression of an intimate relationship with our heavenly Father, who makes his own love and resources available to us.

Psalm 9:1-2 *I will thank you, LORD, with all my heart. . . . I will sing praises to your name, O Most High.*

Through prayer we praise our mighty God.

Does the Bible teach a "right way" to pray?

Nehemiah 1:4 *For days I mourned, fasted, and prayed to the God of heaven.*

Throughout the Bible effective prayer includes elements of adoration, confession, and commitment, as well as requests.

Matthew 6:9 *Pray like this.*

Jesus taught his disciples that prayer is an intimate relationship with the Father that includes a dependency for daily needs, commitment to obedience, and forgiveness of sin.

Luke 18:1 *One day Jesus told his disciples a story to illustrate their need for constant prayer and to show them that they must never give up.*

Prayer is to be consistent and persistent.

Nehemiah 2:4-5 *The king asked, "Well, how can I help you?" With a prayer to the God of heaven, I replied . . .*

Prayer can be spontaneous.

Does God always answer prayer?

James 5:16 *Confess your sins to each other and pray for each other so that you may be healed. The earnest prayer of a righteous person has great power and wonderful results.*

1 John 5:14 *We can be confident that he will listen to us whenever we ask him for anything in line with his will.*

We can be confident of God's response to our prayer when we submit first to his will.

2 Corinthians 12:8-9 *Three different times I begged the Lord to take it away. Each time he said, "My power works best in your weakness."*

Sometimes, like Paul, we find that God answers prayer by giving us not what we ask for but something better.

Exodus 14:15 *The LORD said to Moses, "Why are you crying out to me? Tell the people to get moving!"*
Our prayer must be accompanied by a willingness to obey with our actions.

PROMISE FROM GOD: 1 Peter 3:12 *The eyes of the Lord watch over those who do right, and his ears are open to their prayers.*

PREGNANCY

So many people are giving me advice. How do I know who to listen to?

Colossians 2:8 *Don't let anyone lead you astray with empty philosophy and high-sounding nonsense that come from human thinking.*

Proverbs 16:21 *The wise are known for their understanding, and instruction is appreciated if it's well presented.*
The best advice usually comes from strong Christians who've already experienced the joy and pain of childbearing.

I'm frightened at the thought of labor and delivery. How can I find peace?

Psalm 29:11 *The LORD gives his people strength. The LORD blesses them with peace.*

While labor brings pain, it also draws our eyes heavenward and brings us closer to God. When we openly declare our fears and weakness, he promises to draw near to us.

Does God already know and have a plan for my baby?

Psalm 139:16 *You saw me before I was born. Every day of my life was recorded in your book. Every moment was laid out before a single day had passed.*

Psalm 139:13-15 *You made all the delicate, inner parts of my body and knit me together in my mother's womb. Thank you for making me so wonderfully complex! . . . You watched me as I was being formed in utter seclusion, as I was woven together in the dark of the womb.*

The shaping of a child's life began long before he or she is born, even before conception.

I'm so frightened sometimes. What if something goes wrong?

Psalm 22:9 *You brought me safely from my mother's womb and led me to trust you when I was a nursing infant.*

Philippians 4:6-7 *Don't worry about anything; instead, pray about everything. Tell God what you need, and thank him for all he has done. If you do this, you will experience God's peace, which is far more wonderful than the human mind can understand. His peace will guard your hearts and minds as you live in Christ Jesus.*

1 Peter 5:7 *Give all your worries and cares to God, for he cares about what happens to you.*

Trusting in God takes effort. We must walk with him day by day, learning about his personality and his promises.

Only then will we experience firsthand his unlimited ability to care for our needs.

Will my child grow to love the Lord?

Psalm 22:10 *I was thrust upon you at my birth. You have been my God from the moment I was born.*

Psalm 71:6 *You have been with me from birth; from my mother's womb you have cared for me.*

God's love and salvation are available for even the smallest of his children.

PROMISE FROM GOD: Psalm 103:17-18 *But the love of the LORD remains forever with those who fear him. His salvation extends to the children's children of those who are faithful.*

PRIORITIES

What should be my highest priority?

Mark 12:29-30 *Jesus replied, "The most important commandment is this: 'Hear, O Israel! The Lord our God is the one and only Lord. And you must love the Lord your God with all your heart, all your soul, all your mind, and all your strength.'"*

The priority of priorities is to love God. When we love him, we must also "love the world" that he loves.

How do I put God first in my life?

Matthew 6:32-34 *Your heavenly Father already knows all your needs, and he will give you all you need from day to day if you live for him and make the Kingdom of God your primary concern. So don't worry about tomorrow, for tomorrow will bring its own worries. Today's trouble is enough for today.*

Colossians 3:2 *Let heaven fill your thoughts. Do not think only about things down here on earth.*

Eternity with God is our highest goal; therefore, everything we do today should be done to invest in eternity.

What are some tests to determine my priorities?

Proverbs 3:5-6 *Trust in the LORD with all your heart; do not depend on your own understanding. Seek his will in all you do, and he will direct your paths.*

Haggai 1:9 *You hoped for rich harvests, but they were poor. And when you brought your harvest home, I blew it away. Why? Because my house lies in ruins, says the LORD Almighty, while you are all busy building your own fine houses.*

Luke 12:34 *Wherever your treasure is, there your heart and thoughts will also be.*

Priorities are scales on which our love for God is weighed. We focus on what or whom we love most.

What are some benefits of living with right priorities and some dangers of living with wrong priorities?

Psalm 127:1-2 *Unless the LORD builds a house, the work of the builders is useless. Unless the LORD protects a city, guarding it with sentries will do no good. It is useless for you to work so hard from early morning until late at night, anxiously working for food to eat; for God gives rest to his loved ones.*

Psalm 128:1-4 *How happy are those who fear the LORD—all who follow his ways! You will enjoy the fruit of your labor. How happy you will be! How rich your life! Your wife will be like a fruitful vine, flourishing within your home. And look at all those children! There they sit around your table as vigorous and healthy as young olive trees. That is the LORD's reward for those who fear him.*

Proverbs 14:26 *Those who fear the LORD are secure; he will be a place of refuge for their children.*

The proper priorities bring true happiness, joy, delight, and an abundant life. What more could we ask, especially when we add the love and presence of God?

PROMISE FROM GOD: Proverbs 3:6 *Seek his will in all you do, and he will direct your paths.*

PUNISHMENT

See also DISCIPLINE

How does God's discipline compare to parental discipline?

Hebrews 12:10 *But God's discipline is always right and good for us because it means we will share in his holiness.*

God disciplines us as a loving Father, by both consequences and rebuke. His desire is always to bring us back to him, not to humiliate or hurt us.

Romans 1:26 *That is why God abandoned them to their shameful desires.*

Just as parents sometimes must do, God gives sinners over to the consequences of their own behavior, especially when their sin is intentional and deliberate.

Will we be punished for our sins?

Isaiah 26:21 *The LORD is coming from heaven to punish the people of the earth for their sins.*

Judgment and punishment are promised for all sin.

Isaiah 53:8 *But who among the people realized that he was dying for their sins—that he was suffering their punishment?*

Revelation 6:10 *O Sovereign Lord, holy and true, how long will it be before you judge the people who belong to this world for what they have done to us?*

1 Peter 4:5 *But just remember that they will have to face God, who will judge everyone, both the living and the dead.*

Judgment will surely come upon all who reject Christ.

PROMISE FROM GOD: Romans 3:25 *For God sent Jesus to take the punishment for our sins. . . . We are made right with God when we believe that Jesus shed his blood, sacrificing his life for us.*

PURITY

Why is purity so important?

Psalm 18:20-21 *The LORD rewarded me for doing right; he compensated me because of my innocence. For I have kept the ways of the LORD; I have not turned from my God to follow evil.*

Psalm 24:3-6 *Who may climb the mountain of the LORD? Who may stand in his holy place? Only those whose hands and hearts are pure, who do not worship idols and never tell lies. They will receive the LORD's blessing and have right standing with God their savior. They alone may enter God's presence and worship the God of Israel.*

Matthew 5:8 *God blesses those whose hearts are pure, for they will see God.*

2 Timothy 2:21 *If you keep yourself pure, you will be a utensil God can use for his purpose. Your life will be clean, and you will be ready for the Master to use you for every good work.*

Purity in the Christian life shows an absence of sin. While we can never be fully free of sin in this life, we can strive for that. God honors those who strive for pure hearts because it demonstrates a sincere commitment to be like Jesus.

How can my heart and mind be pure?

Psalm 51:6, 10 *You desire honesty from the heart, so you can teach me to be wise in my inmost being. . . . Create in me a clean heart, O God. Renew a right spirit within me.*

Psalm 86:11 *Teach me your ways, O LORD, that I may live according to your truth! Grant me purity of heart, that I may honor you.*

1 Timothy 1:5 *The purpose of my instruction is that all the Christians there would be filled with love that comes from a pure heart, a clear conscience, and sincere faith.*

1 Peter 1:22 *You can have sincere love for each other as brothers and sisters because you were cleansed from your sins*

when you accepted the truth of the Good News. So see to it that you really do love each other intensely with all your hearts.

Philippians 4:8 *Fix your thoughts on what is true and honorable and right. Think about things that are pure and lovely and admirable. Think about things that are excellent and worthy of praise.*

James 3:17 *The wisdom that comes from heaven is first of all pure.*

When God forgives us, he sees us as pure.

What if I have not been living a pure life?

1 Corinthians 1:30 *God alone made it possible for you to be in Christ Jesus . . . [who] made us pure and holy and . . . gave himself to purchase our freedom.*

Hebrews 9:14 *Just think how much more the blood of Christ will purify our hearts from deeds that lead to death so that we can worship the living God.*

1 John 1:9 *If we confess our sins to him, he is faithful and just to forgive us and to cleanse us from every wrong.*

Psalm 51:2, 7 *Wash me clean from my guilt. Purify me from my sin. . . . Purify me from my sins, and I will be clean; wash me, and I will be whiter than snow.*

Hebrews 10:22 *Let us go right into the presence of God, with true hearts fully trusting him. For our evil consciences have been sprinkled with Christ's blood to make us clean, and our bodies have been washed with pure water.*

Christ saves us from any and all sin. Seek his cleansing, and experience the freedom of a forgiven heart.

PROMISE FROM GOD: Psalm 51:7 *Purify me from my sins, and I will be clean; wash me, and I will be whiter than snow.*

PURPOSE

How can I know God's purpose for my life as a mother?

Joshua 14:12 *If the LORD is with me, I will drive them out of the land, just as the LORD said.*

A vision of God's future allowed Caleb to see his own purpose and not the strength of his enemies.

1 Samuel 17:26 *Who is this pagan Philistine anyway, that he is allowed to defy the armies of the living God?*

While others saw a fearsome giant, David saw an opportunity for God's mighty work.

Nehemiah 2:17 *Let us rebuild the wall of Jerusalem and rid ourselves of this disgrace!*

Nehemiah's passion to rebuild the walls of Jerusalem was rooted in God's purposes for his people.

Philippians 1:20 *For I live in eager expectation and hope . . . that I will always be bold for Christ, . . . and that my life will always honor Christ.*

Philippians 3:12 *I keep working toward that day when I will finally be all that Christ Jesus saved me for and wants me to be.*

Paul's great purpose, whether by life or death, was to win others to Christ.

PROMISE FROM GOD: Psalm 57:2 *I cry out to God Most High, to God who will fulfill his purpose for me.*

RAPE

Where was God, my tower of strength, my refuge? Doesn't he care?

Psalm 10:17 *LORD, you know the hopes of the helpless. Surely you will listen to their cries and comfort them.*

Psalm 55:17 *Morning, noon, and night I plead aloud in my distress, and the LORD hears my voice.*

Psalm 118:5 *In my distress I prayed to the LORD, and the LORD answered me and rescued me.*

Psalm 119:76 *Let your unfailing love comfort me, just as you promised me, your servant.*

We don't know why God allows tragedies to enter our lives, but we do know that God hurts deeply with us and loves us more than we'll ever know. He comforts us and gives us the strength to work through our pain.

Genesis 37:28 *When the traders came by, his brothers pulled Joseph out of the pit and sold him for twenty pieces of silver.*

Sometimes we suffer because of the sins of others and not our own sins.

What is the Lord's response to rape?

Psalm 11:5 *The LORD examines both the righteous and the wicked. He hates everyone who loves violence.*

Psalm 12:5 *The LORD replies, "I have seen violence done to the helpless, and I have heard the groans of the poor. Now I will rise up to rescue them, as they have longed for me to do."*
God hates all violence, and he hates those who love violence. They will surely be severely judged.

Does the victim of a rape share in the blame of the crime?

Deuteronomy 22:25-26 *If the man meets the engaged woman out in the country, and he rapes her, then only the man should die. Do nothing to the young woman; she has committed no crime worthy of death. This case is similar to that of someone who attacks and murders a neighbor.*

Proverbs 16:29 *Violent people deceive their companions, leading them down a harmful path.*

Proverbs 24:2 *They spend their days plotting violence, and their words are always stirring up trouble.*
Rape is a violent act against an innocent victim. There is no excuse for such a terrible crime.

How can I avoid feelings of anger and hatred?

2 Samuel 13:11-15, 21-22, 29 *As she was feeding him, he grabbed her and demanded, "Come to bed with me, my darling sister." "No, my brother!" she cried. "Don't be foolish! Don't do this to me! You know what a serious crime it is to do such a thing in Israel. . . ." But Amnon wouldn't listen to her, and since he was stronger than she was, he raped her. Then suddenly Amnon's love turned to hate. . . . When King David heard what had happened, he was very angry. And though Absalom never spoke to Amnon about it, he hated Amnon deeply because of what he had done to his sister. . . . So at Absalom's signal they murdered Amnon.*

Psalm 37:8 *Stop your anger! Turn from your rage! Do not envy others—it only leads to harm.*

Ephesians 4:31-32 *Get rid of all bitterness, rage, anger, harsh words, and slander, as well as all types of malicious behavior. Instead, be kind to each other, tenderhearted, forgiving one another, just as God through Christ has forgiven you.*

If we fill our hearts and minds with God and his good things, we will empty our hearts and minds of anger, hatred, and plotting violence.

How can the answer possibly be forgiveness?

Matthew 5:44 *I say, love your enemies! Pray for those who persecute you!*

Matthew 18:21-22 *Peter came to him and asked, "Lord, how often should I forgive someone who sins against me? Seven times?" "No!" Jesus replied, "seventy times seven!"*

Mark 11:25 *When you are praying, first forgive anyone you are holding a grudge against, so that your Father in heaven will forgive your sins, too.*

Romans 12:21 *Don't let evil get the best of you, but conquer evil by doing good.*

Christ forgave those who crucified him. There is nothing harder—or more healing—than forgiving someone who has greatly wronged you.

I was raped and now I'm pregnant. How can I possibly love this child?

1 John 4:7 *Let us continue to love one another, for love comes from God. Anyone who loves is born of God and knows God.*

God, the author and creator of life, can fill your heart with love and create goodness, even in the worst of circumstances.

PROMISE FROM GOD: Revelation 21:4 *He will remove all of their sorrows, and there will be no more death or sorrow or crying or pain. For the old world and its evils are gone forever.*

REBELLION

What does it mean to rebel against God?

Numbers 20:12 *Because you did not trust me enough to demonstrate my holiness to the people of Israel, you will not lead them into the land I am giving them!*

Moses rebelled when he disregarded God's instructions for his leadership.

Jeremiah 1:16 *They worship idols that they themselves have made!*

Matthew 6:21 *Wherever your treasure is, there your heart and thoughts will also be.*

We rebel against God whenever we give our devotion to other things.

Judges 2:11-12 *Then the Israelites . . . abandoned the LORD. . . . They chased after other gods, worshiping the gods of the people around them.*

When our rebellion leads to false worship we are in peril of destruction.

Isaiah 59:2 *Your sins have cut you off from God.*

1 John 3:4 *Those who sin are opposed to the law of God.*
Sin is rebellion against God, wanting to do things our way.
When we rebel against God we become separated from
him.

1 Samuel 12:15 *If you rebel against the LORD's commands and refuse to listen to him, then his hand will be
as heavy upon you as it was upon your ancestors.*
Rebellion is refusing to listen to and obey God.

Ezekiel 20:13 *They wouldn't obey my instructions even
though obedience would have given them life.*
Sometimes our rebellion can be so stubborn that we refuse
to obey even when obedience means our very life.

Hebrews 3:12 *Be careful then, dear brothers and sisters.
Make sure that your own hearts are not evil and unbelieving,
turning you away from the living God.*
The ultimate spiritual rebellion is refusing to accept the
gracious offer of salvation through Jesus Christ.

Hosea 11:11 *"I will bring them home again," says the
LORD.*
No matter how far the rebel strays, God still loves him
or her with an everlasting love.

**Isn't a certain amount of rebellion to be expected—
especially in children and teenagers?**
2 Samuel 15:10 *[Absolom] sent secret messengers to every
part of Israel to stir up a rebellion against the king.*
The story of Absalom and David is a classic and heart-
breaking story of the rebellion of son against father.

Ephesians 6:4 *Don't make your children angry by the way you treat them.*

Authority without loving relationship always provokes rebellion.

Is it ever OK for my children to rebel?

1 Peter 4:3 *You have had enough in the past of the evil things that godless people enjoy.*

When under pressure to participate in sinful activities, the Christian is to rebel against the crowd.

Matthew 21:12 *Jesus entered the Temple and began to drive out the merchants.*

Jesus himself rebelled against the systematic corruption of the Temple.

PROMISE FROM GOD: Jeremiah 3:22 *Come back to me, and I will heal your wayward hearts.*

RECONCILIATION

What does the Bible say about reconciliation between people?

Matthew 5:23-24 *If you are standing before the altar in the Temple, offering a sacrifice to God, and you suddenly remember that someone has something against you, leave your sacrifice there beside the altar. Go and be reconciled to that person. Then come and offer your sacrifice to God.*

Being reconciled with other people is important to our relationship with God.

RECONCILIATION

Matthew 5:25-26 *Come to terms quickly with your enemy before it is too late and you are dragged into court, handed over to an officer, and thrown in jail. I assure you that you won't be free again until you have paid the last penny.*

Working for reconciliation with others is very prudent.

Matthew 18:15 *If another believer sins against you, go privately and point out the fault. If the other person listens and confesses it, you have won that person back.*

God wants us to resolve our differences with others.

Ephesians 2:14 *Christ himself has made peace between us Jews and you Gentiles by making us all one people. He has broken down the wall of hostility that used to separate us.*

God, through Christ, has made a way for groups at enmity with one another to make peace and be fully reconciled.

How can we be reconciled to God?

Romans 5:10 *Since we were restored to friendship with God by the death of his Son while we were still his enemies, we will certainly be delivered from eternal punishment by his life.*

Ephesians 2:13 *Now you belong to Christ Jesus. Though you once were far away from God, now you have been brought near to him because of the blood of Christ.*

Isaiah 53:5 *He was wounded and crushed for our sins. He was beaten that we might have peace. He was whipped, and we were healed!*

Colossians 1:20-21 *By him God reconciled everything to himself. He made peace with everything in heaven and on*

earth by means of his blood on the cross. This includes you
who were once so far away from God.

Colossians 2:14 *He canceled the record that contained
the charges against us. He took it and destroyed it by nailing
it to Christ's cross.*

Through the death of the Lord Jesus Christ, God has made
it possible for us to be reconciled to him.

Romans 5:1 *We have been made right in God's sight by
faith.*

2 Corinthians 5:19-21 *God was in Christ, reconciling
the world to himself, no longer counting people's sins against
them. This is the wonderful message he has given us to tell
others. We are Christ's ambassadors, and God is using us to
speak to you. We urge you, as though Christ himself were here
pleading with you, "Be reconciled to God!" For God made
Christ, who never sinned, to be the offering for our sin, so
that we could be made right with God through Christ.*

We must have faith in what Jesus Christ has done for us
in order to be reconciled with God.

PROMISE FROM GOD: Colossians 1:21-22
*You were his enemies, separated from him by your evil
thoughts and actions, yet now he has brought you back as his
friends. He has done this through his death on the cross in his
own human body. As a result, he has brought you into the very
presence of God, and you are holy and blameless as you stand
before him without a single fault.*

REGRETS

How can I deal with the regrets of my life?

Psalm 51:1, 12 *Blot out the stain of my sins. Restore to me again the joy of your salvation.*

Regrets caused by sin are cleansed through heartfelt confession, forgiveness, and repentance.

Ezekiel 6:9-10 *At last they will hate themselves for all their wickedness. They will know that I alone am the LORD.*

God sometimes uses brokenness and remorse to bring true repentance.

How can I avoid regrets in the future?

Matthew 27:3 *When Judas, who had betrayed him, realized that Jesus had been condemned to die, he was filled with remorse.*

Judas's self-destructive regrets were caused by a combination of selfishness and a failure to consider the full consequences of his decision.

2 Samuel 12:13 *David confessed to Nathan, "I have sinned against the LORD."*

God wants us to know that the consequences of sin always include deep regret.

PROMISE FROM GOD: 2 Corinthians 7:10 *God can use sorrow in our lives to help us turn away from sin and seek salvation. We will never regret that kind of sorrow. But sorrow without repentance is the kind that results in death.*

RELATIONSHIPS

See FRIENDSHIP

REMEMBERING

How can remembering God help me in my spiritual walk?

Nehemiah 4:14 *As I looked over the situation, I called together the leaders and the people and said to them, "Don't be afraid of the enemy! Remember the Lord, who is great and glorious, and fight for your friends, your families, and your homes!"*

Remember God as the one who helps you fight and win in life's battles.

Psalm 63:6 *I lie awake thinking of you, meditating on you through the night.*

Remember God day and night. Meditate on him and his great love for you.

Jonah 2:7 *When I had lost all hope, I turned my thoughts once more to the LORD. And my earnest prayer went out to you in your holy Temple.*

Remember God as the source of the hope you think you've lost.

Deuteronomy 8:11, 14 *That is the time to be careful! Beware that in your plenty you do not forget the LORD your God and disobey his commands, regulations, and laws. That is the time to be careful. Do not become proud at that time and forget the LORD your God, who rescued you from slavery in the land of Egypt.*

Remember God when you have plenty, for you will want him when you have little.

Through what other ways does God help me remember him?

Exodus 31:13 *Tell the people of Israel to keep my Sabbath day, for the Sabbath is a sign of the covenant between me and you forever. It helps you to remember that I am the LORD, who makes you holy.*

As we keep the Lord's Day, we remember God's presence.

Genesis 9:16 *When I see the rainbow in the clouds, I will remember the eternal covenant between God and every living creature on earth.*

When we see a rainbow, we remember God's promises.

Luke 22:19 *He took a loaf of bread; and when he had thanked God for it, he broke it in pieces and gave it to the disciples, saying, "This is my body, given for you. Do this in remembrance of me."*

When we eat the Lord's Supper, we remember Christ's sacrifice for us.

2 Peter 1:12-13 *I plan to keep on reminding you of these things—even though you already know them and are standing firm in the truth. Yes, I believe I should keep on reminding you of these things as long as I live.*

When we talk about God with his people, we remember his blessings.

2 Peter 3:1-2 *This is my second letter to you, dear friends, and in both of them I have tried to stimulate your wholesome thinking and refresh your memory. I want you to remember and understand what the holy prophets said long*

ago and what our Lord and Savior commanded through your apostles.

When we read God's Word, we remember who God is and what he has done.

How can I help myself and others make lasting memories of God's work in our lives?

Exodus 16:32 *Moses gave them this command from the LORD: "Take two quarts of manna and keep it forever as a treasured memorial of the LORD's provision. by doing this, later generations will be able to see the bread that the LORD provided in the wilderness when he brought you out of Egypt."*

Joshua 4:6 *We will use these stones to build a memorial. In the future, your children will ask, "What do these stones mean to you?"*

Joshua 22:26-27 *We decided to build the altar, not for burnt sacrifices, but as a memorial. It will remind our descendants and your descendants that we, too, have the right to worship the LORD at his sanctuary with our burnt offerings, sacrifices, and peace offerings.*

Esther 9:28 *These days would be remembered and kept from generation to generation and celebrated by every family throughout the provinces and cities of the empire. These days would never cease to be celebrated among the Jews, nor would the memory of what happened ever die out among their descendants.*

Special days and special objects associated with God's blessings continue to remind us of God's future blessings, too.

PROMISE FROM GOD: Psalm 78:4 *We will not hide these truths from our children but will tell the next generation about the glorious deeds of the LORD. We will tell of his power and the mighty miracles he did.*

*R*ENEWAL

How can I experience renewal in my life?

Psalm 51:10 *Create in me a clean heart, O God. Renew a right spirit within me.*

Jeremiah 31:18 *I have heard Israel saying, "You disciplined me severely, but I deserved it. I was like a calf that needed to be trained for the yoke and plow. Turn me again to you and restore me, for you alone are the LORD my God."*

Ezekiel 36:26-27 *I will give you a new heart with new and right desires, and I will put a new spirit in you. I will take out your stony heart of sin and give you a new, obedient heart. And I will put my Spirit in you so you will obey my laws and do whatever I command.*

Acts 3:19 *Now turn from your sins and turn to God, so you can be cleansed of your sins.*

Ephesians 4:22-24 *Throw off your old evil nature and your former way of life, which is rotten through and through. . . . Instead, there must be a spiritual renewal of your thoughts and attitudes. You must display a new nature because you are a new person, created in God's likeness—righteous, holy, and true.*

Colossians 3:10 *In its place you have clothed yourselves with a brand-new nature that is continually being renewed as you learn more and more about Christ, who created this new nature within you.*

A heart that truly wants to change is a heart that is ready for the renewal that only God's Spirit can bring.

In what ways does God renew me?

Psalm 19:7 *The law of the LORD is perfect, reviving the soul. The decrees of the LORD are trustworthy, making wise the simple.*

God revives my soul.

Psalm 119:25 *I lie in the dust, completely discouraged; revive me by your word.*

God revives me by his word.

Psalm 23:3 *He renews my strength. He guides me along right paths, bringing honor to his name.*

God renews my strength.

Psalm 94:19 *When doubts filled my mind, your comfort gave me renewed hope and cheer.*

God renews my hope.

Psalm 119:40, 93 *I long to obey your commandments! Renew my life with your goodness. I will never forget your commandments, for you have used them to restore my joy and health.*

God restores my joy and health.

2 Corinthians 4:16 *That is why we never give up. Though our bodies are dying, our spirits are being renewed every day.*

God renews our spirits.

PROMISE FROM GOD: Psalm 23:3 *He renews my strength. He guides me along right paths, bringing honor to his name.*

REPENTANCE

Why does God want us to repent?

Leviticus 26:40 *At last my people will confess their sins and the sins of their ancestors for betraying me and being hostile toward me.*

All of us need to repent because we have betrayed God with our sins.

2 Chronicles 30:9 *The LORD your God is gracious and merciful. If you return to him, he will not continue to turn his face from you.*

Repentance is necessary for an ongoing relationship with God.

Proverbs 28:13 *People who cover over their sins will not prosper. But if they confess and forsake them, they will receive mercy.*

Isaiah 55:7 *Let the people turn from their wicked deeds. Let them banish from their minds the very thought of doing wrong! Let them turn to the LORD that he may have mercy on them. Yes, turn to our God, for he will abundantly pardon.*

Jeremiah 3:12 *Go and say these words to Israel, "This is what the LORD says: O Israel, my faithless people, come home to me again, for I am merciful. I will not be angry with you forever."*

Repentance is necessary to receive God's mercy.

Ezekiel 18:30-32 *I will judge each of you, O people of Israel, according to your actions, says the Sovereign LORD. Turn from your sins! Don't let them destroy you! Put all your rebellion behind you, and get for yourselves a new heart and a new spirit. For why should you die, O people of Israel? I don't want you to die, says the Sovereign LORD. Turn back and live!*

Ezekiel 33:11 *As surely as I live, says the Sovereign LORD, I take no pleasure in the death of wicked people. I only want them to turn from their wicked ways so they can live. Turn! Turn from your wickedness, O people of Israel! Why should you die?*

Repentance is the key to having new life from God.

Matthew 3:2 *Turn from your sins and turn to God, because the Kingdom of Heaven is near.*

Luke 24:47 *There is forgiveness of sins for all who turn to me.*

Acts 2:37-38 *Peter's words convicted them deeply, and they said to him and to the other apostles, "Brothers, what should we do?" Peter replied, "Each of you must turn from your sins and turn to God, and be baptized in the name of Jesus Christ for the forgiveness of your sins. Then you will receive the gift of the Holy Spirit."*

Forgiveness of sins and entrance to the kingdom of heaven is only for those who have turned away from their sins and turned to God.

Matthew 11:20-23 *Jesus began to denounce the cities where he had done most of his miracles, because they hadn't turned from their sins and turned to God. . . . "You people of Capernaum, will you be exalted to heaven? No, you will be brought down to the place of the dead."*

Refusal to turn away from our sins will bring God's judgment.

PROMISE FROM GOD: 2 Chronicles 7:14
*If my people who are called by my name will humble
themselves and pray and seek my face and turn from their
wicked ways, I will hear from heaven and will forgive their
sins and heal their land.*

RESENTMENT

What causes feelings of resentment?

2 Samuel 6:16 *As the Ark of the LORD entered the City
of David, Michal, the daughter of Saul, looked down from
her window. When she saw King David leaping and dancing
before the LORD, she was filled with contempt for him.*

Disagreement over conduct can cause resentment.

Genesis 27:36 *Esau said bitterly, "No wonder his name is
Jacob, for he has deceived me twice, first taking my birthright
and now stealing my blessing. Oh, haven't you saved even one
blessing for me?"*

Being deceived can cause resentment.

Genesis 4:3-5, 8 *At harvesttime Cain brought to the
LORD a gift of his farm produce, while Abel brought several
choice lambs from the best of his flock. The LORD accepted
Abel and his offering, but he did not accept Cain and his
offering. This made Cain very angry and dejected. . . . Later
Cain suggested to his brother, Abel, "Let's go out into the
fields." And while they were together there, Cain attacked
and killed his brother.*

Jealousy can cause resentment.

Luke 15:27-30 *"Your brother is back," he was told, "and your father has killed the calf we were fattening and has prepared a great feast. We are celebrating because of his safe return." The older brother was angry and wouldn't go in. His father came out and begged him, but he replied, "All these years I've worked hard for you and never once refused to do a single thing you told me to. And in all that time you never gave me even one young goat for a feast with my friends. Yet when this son of yours comes back after squandering your money on prostitutes, you celebrate by killing the finest calf we have."*

Feeling left out can cause resentment.

Genesis 37:2-4 *When Joseph was seventeen years old, he often tended his father's flocks with his half brothers, the sons of his father's wives Bilhah and Zilpah. But Joseph reported to his father some of the bad things his brothers were doing. Now Jacob loved Joseph more than any of his other children because Joseph had been born to him in his old age. So one day he gave Joseph a special gift—a beautiful robe. But his brothers hated Joseph because of their father's partiality. They couldn't say a kind word to him.*

Favoritism can cause resentment.

How do I handle my feelings of resentment?

Proverbs 10:12 *Hatred stirs up quarrels, but love covers all offenses.*

Mark 11:25 *When you are praying, first forgive anyone you are holding a grudge against, so that your Father in heaven will forgive your sins, too.*

Ephesians 4:26-27, 31-32 *"Don't sin by letting anger gain control over you." Don't let the sun go down while you are still angry, for anger gives a mighty foothold to the Devil. Get rid of all bitterness, rage, anger, harsh words, and slander, as well as all types of malicious behavior. Instead, be kind to each other, tenderhearted, forgiving one another, just as God through Christ has forgiven you.*

1 Thessalonians 5:15 *See that no one pays back evil for evil, but always try to do good to each other and to everyone else.*

James 5:9 *Don't grumble about each other, my brothers and sisters, or God will judge you. For look! The great Judge is coming. He is standing at the door!*

If resentment has built up, build up love and forgiveness until they overcome resentment.

PROMISE FROM GOD: Mark 11:25 *When you are praying, first forgive anyone you are holding a grudge against, so that your Father in heaven will forgive your sins, too.*

ℛESPECT

How do I show respect to God?

Leviticus 19:30 *Show reverence toward my sanctuary, for I am the LORD.*

Deuteronomy 10:12 *And now, Israel, what does the LORD your God require of you? He requires you to fear him, to live according to his will, to love and worship him with all your heart and soul.*

2 Kings 17:36 *Worship only the LORD, who brought you out of Egypt with such mighty miracles and power. You must worship him and bow before him; offer sacrifices to him alone.*

Psalm 96:7-9 *O nations of the world, recognize the LORD; recognize that the LORD is glorious and strong. Give to the LORD the glory he deserves! Bring your offering and come to worship him. Worship the LORD in all his holy splendor. Let all the earth tremble before him.*

Hebrews 12:28-29 *Since we are receiving a Kingdom that cannot be destroyed, let us be thankful and please God by worshiping him with holy fear and awe. For our God is a consuming fire.*

We should show our respect for God by serving and worshiping him with reverence.

Psalm 22:23 *Praise the LORD, all you who fear him! Honor him, all you descendants of Jacob! Show him reverence, all you descendants of Israel!*

Isaiah 33:13 *You that are near, acknowledge my might!*

Revelation 19:5 *Praise our God, all his servants, from the least to the greatest, all who fear him.*

One way to show God our respect is by praising him for what he has done and for who he is.

Ecclesiastes 5:1 *As you enter the house of God, keep your ears open and your mouth shut!*

Habakkuk 2:20 *The LORD is in his holy Temple. Let all the earth be silent before him.*

Zephaniah 1:7 *Stand in silence in the presence of the Sovereign LORD.*

Keeping silence in God's presence shows respect for him.

Exodus 20:20 *"Don't be afraid," Moses said, "for God has come in this way to show you his awesome power. From now on, let your fear of him keep you from sinning!"*
Our reverence for God should keep us from sinning.

Leviticus 22:32 *Do not treat my holy name as common and ordinary. I must be treated as holy by the people of Israel. It is I, the LORD, who makes you holy.*
Respect for God means that we show reverence for his name.

Psalm 115:11 *All you who fear the LORD, trust the LORD! He is your helper; he is your shield.*
When we trust in God, we show that we truly respect him.

Ecclesiastes 12:13 *Here is my final conclusion: Fear God and obey his commands, for this is the duty of every person.*
Obedience to God is a way to respect him.

2 Chronicles 19:6 *Always think carefully before pronouncing judgment.*
Remember that you do not judge to please people but to please the Lord.

Nehemiah 5:15 *This was quite a contrast to the former governors who had laid heavy burdens on the people, demanding a daily ration of food and wine, besides a pound of silver. Even their assistants took advantage of the people. But because of my fear of God, I did not act that way.*
If we truly respect God, we should treat other people with fairness and justice.

Acts 10:2 *He was a devout man who feared the God of Israel, as did his entire household. He gave generously to charity.*
Giving to charity is a way to show our reverence for God.

PROMISE FROM GOD: Psalm 33:18 *The LORD watches over those who fear him.*

RIGHTEOUSNESS

What is righteousness?

Genesis 6:9 *Noah was a righteous man, the only blameless man living on earth at the time. He consistently followed God's will and enjoyed a close relationship with him.*

Romans 4:3, 22 *The Scriptures tell us, "Abraham believed God, so God declared him to be righteous." . . . And because of Abraham's faith, God declared him to be righteous.*

Job 1:1 *There was a man named Job who lived in the land of Uz. He was blameless, a man of complete integrity. He feared God and stayed away from evil.*

Righteousness is consistently following God's will, walking with God daily, having an unwavering faith in God and his promises, loving him deeply, demonstrating complete integrity, fearing God, and avoiding evil.

How can I be considered righteous?

Romans 1:17 *This Good News tells us how God makes us right in his sight. This is accomplished from start to finish by faith. As the Scriptures say, "It is through faith that a righteous person has life."*

Romans 3:22 *We are made right in God's sight when we trust in Jesus Christ to take away our sins. And we all can be saved in this same way, no matter who we are or what we have done.*

Romans 5:1-2 *Since we have been made right in God's sight by faith, we have peace with God because of what Jesus Christ our Lord has done for us. Because of our faith, Christ has brought us into this place of highest privilege where we now stand, and we confidently and joyfully look forward to sharing God's glory.*

Romans 10:10 *It is by believing in your heart that you are made right with God, and it is by confessing with your mouth that you are saved.*

2 Corinthians 5:21 *God made Christ, who never sinned, to be the offering for our sin, so that we could be made right with God through Christ.*

Philippians 3:9 *I no longer count on my own goodness or my ability to obey God's law, but I trust Christ to save me. For God's way of making us right with himself depends on faith.*

I am considered righteous before God by trusting in Jesus Christ as my Savior.

How can I pursue and practice righteousness?

Proverbs 21:21 *Whoever pursues godliness and unfailing love will find life, godliness, and honor.*

Matthew 25:37-40 *These righteous ones will reply, "Lord, when did we ever see you hungry and feed you? Or thirsty and give you something to drink? Or a stranger and show you hospitality? Or naked and give you clothing? When did we ever see you sick or in prison, and visit you?" And the King will tell them, "I assure you, when you did it to one of the least of these my brothers and sisters, you were doing it to me!"*

1 Timothy 6:11 *You, Timothy, belong to God; so run from all these evil things, and follow what is right and good. Pursue a godly life, along with faith, love, perseverance, and gentleness.*

1 John 3:7 *Dear children, don't let anyone deceive you about this: When people do what is right, it is because they are righteous, even as Christ is righteous.*

PROMISE FROM GOD: Romans 3:22 *We are made right in God's sight when we trust in Jesus Christ to take away our sins. And we all can be saved in this same way, no matter who we are or what we have done.*

ROUTINE

See BOREDOM

SALVATION

What does it mean to be saved?

Romans 4:8 *What joy for those whose sin is no longer counted against them by the Lord.*

Romans 3:24 *Now God in his gracious kindness declares us not guilty.*

Being saved means no longer having our sins count against us but rather being forgiven by the grace of God.

Psalm 103:12 *He has removed our rebellious acts as far away from us as the east is from the west.*

Being saved means that our sins have been completely removed.

Psalm 51:9-10 *Remove the stain of my guilt. Create in me a clean heart, O God.*

Being saved means that the stain of guilt has been washed away.

1 Peter 2:10 *Once you received none of God's mercy; now you have received his mercy.*

Romans 3:24 *He has done this through Christ, who has freed us by taking away our sins.*

Being saved means that we are forgiven in Christ.

How can I be saved?

Romans 10:13 *Anyone who calls on the name of the Lord will be saved.*

God's Word promises salvation to anyone who calls on Jesus' name.

John 3:16 *God so loved the world that he gave his only Son, so that everyone who believes in him will not perish but have eternal life.*

John 5:24 *I assure you, those who listen to my message and believe in God who sent me have eternal life.*

Jesus himself promised that those who believe in him will be saved.

Is salvation available to anyone?

John 3:16 *For God so loved the world that he gave his only Son, so that everyone who believes in him will not perish but have eternal life.*

Anyone can receive salvation by believing in Jesus Christ and his message of Good News.

Hebrews 9:27 *It is destined that each person dies only once and after that comes judgment.*

Salvation is available to all, but a time will come when it will be too late to receive it.

How can I be sure of my salvation?

John 1:12 *But to all who believed him and accepted him, he gave the right to become children of God.*

Just as a child cannot be unborn, a child of God cannot be un-born-again.

Romans 8:14 *All who are led by the Spirit of God are children of God.*

The Holy Spirit takes up residence in our hearts and assures us that we are God's children.

Matthew 14:30-31 *"Save me, Lord!" he shouted. Instantly Jesus reached out his hand and grabbed him.*

We cannot save ourselves from sin, guilt, judgment, and spiritual death. Only Jesus Christ can save us.

Why is salvation so central to Christianity?

Genesis 6:11-13 *The earth had become corrupt in God's sight . . . So God said to Noah, "I have decided to destroy all living creatures."*

Romans 6:23 *The wages of sin is death.*

Salvation is necessary because sin against a holy God separates us from him, bringing judgment and spiritual death.

Exodus 12:23 *When he sees the blood on the top and sides of the doorframe, the LORD will pass over your home. He will not permit the Destroyer to enter and strike down your firstborn.*

Salvation through Christ is dramatically foreshadowed through the Passover lamb.

Acts 4:12 *There is salvation in no one else! There is no other name in all of heaven for people to call on to save them.*

Although it may sound exclusive, the Bible's claim of one way to salvation is actually an expression of the grace and kindness of God.

PROMISE FROM GOD: Romans 10:9 *If you confess with your mouth that Jesus is Lord and believe in your heart that God raised him from the dead, you will be saved.*

SATISFACTION

See CONTENTMENT

SECURITY

How does my faith help me feel secure?

Psalm 40:1-2 *I waited patiently for the LORD to help me, and he turned to me and heard my cry. He lifted me out of the pit of despair, out of the mud and the mire. He set my feet on solid ground and steadied me as I walked along.*

Psalm 125:1 *Those who trust in the LORD are as secure as Mount Zion; they will not be defeated but will endure forever.*

Proverbs 1:33 *All who listen to me will live in peace and safety, unafraid of harm.*

Matthew 7:24-25 *Anyone who listens to my teaching and obeys me is wise, like a person who builds a house on solid rock. Though the rain comes in torrents and the floodwaters rise and the winds beat against that house, it won't collapse, because it is built on rock.*

The Christian's safety and security are rooted deeply in the Lord's presence. With him we can face life with great courage. Without him we stand alone.

How does God provide security?

Psalm 3:3 *You, O LORD, are a shield around me, my glory, and the one who lifts my head high.*

Psalm 9:9-10 *The LORD is a shelter for the oppressed, a refuge in times of trouble. Those who know your name trust in you, for you, O LORD, have never abandoned anyone who searches for you.*

Psalm 46:1-3 *God is our refuge and strength, always ready to help in times of trouble. So we will not fear, even if earthquakes come and the mountains crumble into the sea. Let the oceans roar and foam. Let the mountains tremble as the waters surge!*

Psalm 57:1 *Have mercy on me, O God, have mercy! I look to you for protection. I will hide beneath the shadow of your wings until this violent storm is past.*

Psalm 63:8 *I follow close behind you; your strong right hand holds me securely.*

Proverbs 14:26 *Those who fear the LORD are secure; he will be a place of refuge for their children.*

Proverbs 18:10 *The name of the LORD is a strong fortress; the godly run to him and are safe.*

No matter how much the storms of life batter us, we are eternally secure with God. Nothing can ever separate us from his presence.

How can I feel secure about eternity?

Romans 8:38-39 *I am convinced that nothing can ever separate us from his love. Death can't, and life can't. The angels can't, and the demons can't. Our fears for today, our worries about tomorrow, and even the powers of hell can't keep God's love away. Whether we are high above the sky or in the deepest ocean, nothing in all creation will ever be able to separate us from the love of God that is revealed in Christ Jesus our Lord.*

2 Corinthians 1:22 *He has identified us as his own by placing the Holy Spirit in our hearts as the first installment of everything he will give us.*

Titus 3:7 *He declared us not guilty because of his great kindness.*

And now we know that we will inherit eternal life.

1 Peter 1:4-5 *God has reserved a priceless inheritance for his children. It is kept in heaven for you, pure and undefiled, beyond the reach of change and decay. And God, in his mighty power, will protect you until you receive this salvation, because you are trusting him. It will be revealed on the last day for all to see.*

1 John 5:18 *We know that those who have become part of God's family do not make a practice of sinning, for God's Son holds them securely, and the evil one cannot get his hands on them.*

Revelation 3:5 *All who are victorious will be clothed in white. I will never erase their names from the Book of Life, but I will announce before my Father and his angels that they are mine.*

God has promised to save us when we accept his Son, Jesus Christ, as our Savior. God always keeps his promises.

PROMISE FROM GOD: Titus 3:7 *He declared us not guilty because of his great kindness. And now we know that we will inherit eternal life.*

$\mathcal{S}$ELF-ESTEEM

See WORTH/WORTHINESS

$\mathcal{S}$ERVICE

What are some requirements for serving God?

Psalm 2:11 *Serve the LORD with reverent fear, and rejoice with trembling.*

A willing heart and reverent awe of God

Psalm 101:6 *I will keep a protective eye on the godly, so they may dwell with me in safety. Only those who are above reproach will be allowed to serve me.*

A desire to please God and walk in his ways

Matthew 6:24 *No one can serve two masters. For you will hate one and love the other, or be devoted to one and despise the other. You cannot serve both God and money.*

Loyalty to God

Romans 7:6 *We have been released from the law, for we died with Christ, and we are no longer captive to its power. Now we can really serve God, not in the old way by obeying the letter of the law, but in the new way, by the Spirit.*

A desire to be led by the Holy Spirit

Acts 20:19 *I have done the Lord's work humbly—yes, and with tears. I have endured the trials that came to me from the plots of the Jews.*

Humility

Galatians 5:13 *You have been called to live in freedom— not freedom to satisfy your sinful nature, but freedom to serve one another in love.*

Love for others

How should we serve God?

Joshua 22:5 *Be very careful to obey all the commands and the law that Moses gave to you. Love the LORD your God, walk in all his ways, obey his commands, be faithful to him, and serve him with all your heart and all your soul.*

Obey and love God.

Joshua 24:15 *Choose today whom you will serve. . . . But as for me and my family, we will serve the LORD.*

Honor God and worship him only.

1 Corinthians 12:4-5 *There are different kinds of spiritual gifts, but it is the same Holy Spirit who is the source of them all. There are different kinds of service in the church, but it is the same Lord we are serving.*

Exercise your spiritual gifts.

Matthew 25:40 *The King will tell them, "I assure you, when you did it to one of the least of these my brothers and sisters, you were doing it to me!"*

Demonstrate love and kindness to all people, especially those in need.

Romans 12:11 *Never be lazy in your work, but serve the Lord enthusiastically.*

Serve enthusiastically.

How did Jesus serve?

Matthew 20:26-28 *Among you it should be quite different. Whoever wants to be a leader among you must be your servant. . . . For even I, the Son of Man, came here not to be served but to serve others, and to give my life as a ransom for many.*

He gave his life for us.

Philippians 2:7 *He made himself nothing; he took the humble position of a slave and appeared in human form.*

He humbled himself.

Matthew 20:32 *Jesus stopped in the road and called, "What do you want me to do for you?"*

He served people who needed him.

John 13:4-5, 14-15 *He got up from the table, took off his robe, wrapped a towel around his waist, and poured water into a basin. Then he began to wash the disciples' feet and to wipe them with the towel he had around him. "Since I, the Lord and Teacher, have washed your feet, you ought to wash each other's feet. I have given you an example to follow. Do as I have done to you."*

He washed his disciples' feet.

How can I have a servant heart?

Philippians 2:5-9 *Your attitude should be the same that Christ Jesus had. Though he was God, he did not demand and cling to his rights as God. He made himself nothing; he took the humble position of a slave and appeared in human form. And in human form he obediently humbled himself even further by dying a criminal's death on a cross. Because of this, God raised him up to the heights of heaven and gave him a name that is above every other name.*

By humbling ourselves as Christ did, obediently doing what God wants

Romans 6:13 *Use your whole body as a tool to do what is right for the glory of God.*

By submitting ourselves to Christ and remaining pure

Genesis 24:18-20 *"Certainly, sir," she said, and she quickly lowered the jug for him to drink. When he had finished, she said, "I'll draw water for your camels, too, until they have had enough!" So she quickly emptied the jug into the watering trough and ran down to the well again. She kept carrying water to the camels until they had finished drinking.*

By helping others who need us

Luke 1:38 *Mary responded, "I am the Lord's servant, and I am willing to accept whatever he wants. May everything you have said come true." And then the angel left.*

By doing what God asks us to do

≣PROMISE FROM GOD: Mark 10:43-44
Among you it should be quite different. Whoever wants to be a leader among you must be your servant, and whoever wants to be first must be the slave of all.

SICKNESS

See HEALTH and HEALING

SINGLE PARENTING

What if I am a single parent or grew up in a single-parent home?

Psalm 68:5 *Father to the fatherless, defender of widows—this is God.*

God has a special place in his heart for those who are lonely or abandoned.

Matthew 28:20 *I am with you always, even to the end of the age.*

God is always with us.

How can I meet the challenges of raising children alone?

Philippians 4:13 *For I can do everything with the help of Christ who gives me the strength I need.*

How do I meet the needs of my hurting children when I'm still dealing with my own pain?

1 Kings 19:11-12 *After the wind there was an earthquake, but the LORD was not in the earthquake. And after the earthquake there was a fire, but the LORD was not in the fire. And after the fire there was the sound of a gentle whisper.*

When you're feeling overwhelmed, take time out to just be with your children. Learn together that calmness in the midst of chaotic circumstances is possible with God's help.

Seize every small opportunity you can find to slow down and listen for his gentle voice.

Hebrews 12:15 *Look after each other so that none of you will miss out on the special favor of God. Watch out that no bitter root of unbelief rises up among you, for whenever it springs up, many are corrupted by its poison.*

In the emotional upheaval that usually accompanies the breakup of a family, watch your words carefully, especially when you talk about your ex-husband. By protecting your children's ears and hearts, you will help their healing process.

Mark 4:39 *When he woke up, he rebuked the wind and said to the water, "Quiet down!" Suddenly the wind stopped, and there was a great calm.*

It's during life's fiercest storms that we learn to rely fully on God. No matter how big the struggle, don't let go of him. He can be trusted to provide for your family.

PROMISE FROM GOD: Isaiah 54:5 *Your Creator will be your husband. The LORD Almighty is his name! He is your Redeemer, the Holy One of Israel, the God of all the earth.*

$\mathscr{S}$PIRITUAL WARFARE

What does the Bible say about spiritual warfare?

1 Peter 5:8 *Be careful! Watch out for attacks from the Devil, your great enemy.*

We must be alert at all times for the sneak attacks of the evil one.

James 4:7 *Resist the Devil, and he will flee from you.*
When we resist the devil in the name and power of Jesus,
he must flee from us.

Matthew 4:4 *Jesus told him, "No! The Scriptures say . . ."*
When under attack by the tempter, Jesus relied on the
Word of God to resist the lies of his adversary.

PROMISE FROM GOD: Ephesians 6:11 *Put
on all of God's armor so that you will be able to stand firm
against all strategies and tricks of the Devil.*

$\mathscr{S}$TRESS

What causes stress?

Genesis 3:6, 23 *She ate some of the fruit. She also gave
some to her husband. . . . Then he ate it, too. . . . So the LORD
God banished Adam and his wife from the Garden of Eden.*

2 Samuel 11:4; 12:13-14 *Then David sent for her;
and when she came to the palace, he slept with her. . . .
Nathan replied, ". . . The LORD has forgiven you, and you
won't die for this sin. But . . . your child will die."*

Luke 22:56-57, 61-62 *She said, "This man was one of
Jesus' followers!" Peter denied it. "Woman," he said, "I don't
even know the man!" . . . At that moment the Lord turned
and looked at Peter. . . . And Peter left the courtyard, crying
bitterly.*

Often stress is of our own doing. When we sin, we bring
the stress of painful consequences upon us.

STRESS

Exodus 16:2-3 *The whole community of Israel spoke bitterly against Moses and Aaron. "Oh, that we were back in Egypt," they moaned.*
Stress comes when we fail to trust God for help.

How can I deal with stress and pressure?

2 Samuel 22:7 *In my distress I cried out to the LORD. . . . He heard me from his sanctuary; my cry reached his ears.*

Psalm 55:22 *Give your burdens to the LORD, and he will take care of you. He will not permit the godly to slip and fall.*

Psalm 62:2 *He alone is my rock and my salvation, my fortress where I will never be shaken.*

Psalm 86:7 *I will call to you whenever trouble strikes, and you will answer me.*

Isaiah 41:10 *Don't be afraid, for I am with you. Do not be dismayed, for I am your God. I will strengthen you. I will help you. I will uphold you with my victorious right hand.*

Matthew 11:28 *Come to me, all of you who are weary and carry heavy burdens, and I will give you rest.*

John 14:1 *Don't be troubled. You trust God, now trust in me.*

2 Corinthians 4:9 *We are hunted down, but God never abandons us. We get knocked down, but we get up again and keep going.*

Galatians 6:9 *Don't get tired of doing what is good. Don't get discouraged and give up, for we will reap a harvest of blessing at the appropriate time.*

Philippians 2:4 *Don't think only about your own affairs, but be interested in others, too, and what they are doing.*

Hebrews 2:18 *Since he himself has gone through suffering and temptation, he is able to help us when we are being tempted.*

PROMISE FROM GOD: John 16:33 *I have told you all this so that you may have peace in me. Here on earth you will have many trials and sorrows. But take heart, because I have overcome the world.*

SUBMISSION

What is submission to God?

Genesis 12:1, 4 *The LORD told Abram, "Leave your country, your relatives, and your father's house, and go to the land that I will show you. . . . So Abram departed as the LORD had instructed him.*

Exodus 7:6 *Moses and Aaron did just as the LORD had commanded them.*

Matthew 26:39, 42 *He went on a little farther and fell face down on the ground, praying, "My Father! If it is possible, let this cup of suffering be taken away from me. Yet I want your will, not mine." . . . Again he left them and prayed, "My Father! If this cup cannot be taken away until I drink it, your will be done."*

John 18:11 *Jesus said to Peter, "Put your sword back into its sheath. Shall I not drink from the cup the Father has given me?"*

Hebrews 5:7-9 *While Jesus was here on earth, he offered prayers and pleadings, with a loud cry and tears, to the one who could deliver him out of death. And God heard his prayers because of his reverence for God. So even though Jesus was God's Son, he learned obedience from the things he suffered. In this way, God qualified him as a perfect High Priest, and he became the source of eternal salvation for all those who obey him.*

Submission to God is obedience to God; doing what he commands.

Why is submission important? What are the benefits of submission?

Proverbs 29:18 *When people do not accept divine guidance, they run wild. But whoever obeys the law is happy.*

Matthew 20:27 *Whoever wants to be first must become your slave.*

Hebrews 2:9 *What we do see is Jesus, who "for a little while was made lower than the angels" and now is "crowned with glory and honor" because he suffered death for us. Yes, by God's grace, Jesus tasted death for everyone in all the world.*

Submitting ourselves to God our Protector keeps us from submitting to the destructive forces of evil.

How should I submit?

Romans 6:13 *Do not let any part of your body become a tool of wickedness, to be used for sinning. Instead, give yourselves completely to God since you have been given new life. And use your whole body as a tool to do what is right for the glory of God.*

Submit your body to God so that he will protect you.

Matthew 26:39 *He went on a little farther and fell face down on the ground, praying, "My Father! If it is possible, let this cup of suffering be taken away from me. Yet I want your will, not mine."*

Submit yourself to God's will so that you can be in touch with God's great plan for you.

Hebrews 12:9 *Since we respect our earthly fathers who disciplined us, should we not all the more cheerfully submit to the discipline of our heavenly Father and live forever?*

Submit to authority and discipline so that you will be spared from foolish behavior.

Ephesians 5:21-22 *You will submit to one another out of reverence for Christ. You wives will submit to your husbands as you do to the Lord.*

Submit to each other in marriage so that you will build each other up and encourage each other.

Hebrews 13:17 *Obey your spiritual leaders and do what they say. Their work is to watch over your souls, and they know they are accountable to God. Give them reason to do this joyfully and not with sorrow. That would certainly not be for your benefit.*

Submit to spiritual leaders so that they can guide you.

Romans 13:1 *Obey the government, for God is the one who put it there. All governments have been placed in power by God.*

Submit to government, for God gave leaders their authority.

Titus 3:1 *Remind your people to submit to the government and its officers. They should be obedient, always ready to do what is good.*

Titus 2:9-10 *Slaves must obey their masters and do their best to please them. They must not talk back or steal, but they must show themselves to be entirely trustworthy and good. Then they will make the teaching about God our Savior attractive in every way.*

Submit to your leaders, and pray for wisdom for them.

What are some ways to show submission?

Romans 12:10 *Love each other with genuine affection, and take delight in honoring each other.*

Love and honor each other.

Philippians 2:3-4 *Don't be selfish; don't live to make a good impression on others. Be humble, thinking of others as better than yourself. Don't think only about your own affairs, but be interested in others, too, and what they are doing.*

Be humble toward others, and honor them as yourself.

James 3:17 *The wisdom that comes from heaven is first of all pure. It is also peace loving, gentle at all times, and willing to yield to others. It is full of mercy and good deeds. It shows no partiality and is always sincere.*

Love peace, be gentle, show mercy, and do good deeds.

PROMISE FROM GOD: Exodus 19:5 *If you will obey me and keep my covenant, you will be my own special treasure from among all the nations of the earth; for all the earth belongs to me.*

$\mathscr{S}$UCCESS

I want to be a successful mother. What is true success in God's eyes?

Acts 16:31 *Believe on the Lord Jesus and you will be saved.*

Faith in Jesus.

Matthew 22:37 *Jesus replied, "You must love the Lord your God with all your heart, all your soul, and all your mind."*

Love for God.

Psalm 119:115 *I intend to obey the commands of my God.*

1 Kings 2:3 *Observe the requirements of the LORD your God and follow all his ways.*

Obedience to God's Word.

Matthew 20:26 *But among you it should be quite different. Whoever wants to be a leader among you must be your servant.*

Serving and helping others.

Jeremiah 37:15-16 *They were furious with Jeremiah and had him flogged and imprisoned. . . . Jeremiah was put into a dungeon cell, where he remained for many days.*

Proverbs 16:3 *Commit your work to the LORD, and then your plans will succeed.*

Committing all you do to God. Putting God first in your life.

Mark 4:19 *All too quickly the message is crowded out by the cares of this life, the lure of wealth, and the desire for nice things.*

True success, that which comes from God, is killed by our attraction to worldly things. When we lust for money, position, power, or fame, we will be tempted to spend our energies to get these things, and that will take us away from a pursuit of God.

Is it OK to try to be successful in this life?

Proverbs 12:24 *Work hard and become a leader; be lazy and become a slave.*

Proverbs 22:29 *Do you see any truly competent workers? They will serve kings rather than ordinary people.*

There are many godly character traits that, if applied to life, often bring material success (hard work, integrity, commitment, serving others, planning).

Genesis 39:2-3 *The LORD was with Joseph and blessed him greatly as he served in the home of his Egyptian master . . . giving him success in everything he did.*

Exodus 33:14 *And the LORD replied, "I will personally go with you . . . everything will be fine for you."*

Throughout the Scriptures, there are frequent references to God's blessings for his people. God allows his people to have material blessing, but urges them never to sacrifice spiritual matters for worldly wealth.

PROMISES FROM GOD: Psalm 60:12 *With God's help we will do mighty things.*

Psalm 84:11 *No good thing will the LORD withhold from those who do what is right.*

UFFERING

Why am I suffering? Doesn't God care about me?

Genesis 37:28 *When the traders came by, his brothers pulled Joseph out of the pit and sold him for twenty pieces of silver.*

Jeremiah 32:18 *You are loving and kind to thousands, though children suffer for their parents' sins.*

Sometimes we suffer because of the sins of others and not because of our own sins.

John 9:2-3 *"Teacher," his disciples asked him, "why was this man born blind? Was it a result of his own sins or those of his parents?" "It was not because of his sins or his parents' sins," Jesus answered.*

Sometimes the suffering that comes to us is not our fault. It just happens. In this case, how we react to the suffering is the key.

Genesis 3:6, 23 *The fruit looked so fresh and delicious . . . she ate some of the fruit. . . . So the LORD God banished Adam and his wife from the Garden of Eden.*

Leviticus 26:43 *At last the people will receive the due punishment for their sins, for they rejected my regulations and despised my laws.*

Proverbs 3:11-12 *My child, don't ignore it when the LORD disciplines you. . . . For the LORD corrects those he loves, just as a father corrects a child in whom he delights.*

Sometimes God sends suffering as a consequence of our sins. He disciplines us because he loves us and wants to correct us and restore us to him.

Deuteronomy 8:2 *Remember how the LORD God led you through the wilderness for forty years, humbling you and testing you . . . to find out whether or not you would really obey his commands?*
Sometimes God tests us with suffering to encourage us to obey him.

1 Peter 4:14 *Be happy if you are insulted for being a Christian, for then the glorious Spirit of God will come upon you.*
Sometimes we willingly suffer because we must take a stand for Christ.

James 1:3 *When your faith is tested, your endurance has a chance to grow.*
Sometimes we willingly suffer because it will help us grow and mature.

2 Timothy 3:12 *Everyone who wants to live a godly life in Christ Jesus will suffer persecution.*
The world hates Christ, so when we identify with him, we can expect the world that inflicted suffering on him to also inflict suffering on us.

Can any good come from suffering?

Job 5:17-18 *Consider the joy of those corrected by God! Do not despise the chastening of the Almighty when you sin. For though he wounds, he also bandages. He strikes, but his hands also heal.*
Suffering, or woundedness, can bring great renewal and healing.

Romans 5:3-4 *We can rejoice, too, when we run into problems and trials, for we know that they are good for us—*

they help us learn to endure. And endurance develops strength of character.

2 Corinthians 1:5 *You can be sure that the more we suffer for Christ, the more God will shower us with his comfort through Christ.*

2 Corinthians 12:10 *Since I know it is all for Christ's good, I am quite content with my weaknesses and with insults, hardships, persecutions, and calamities. For when I am weak, then I am strong.*

2 Timothy 2:10 *I am willing to endure anything if it will bring salvation and eternal glory in Christ Jesus to those God has chosen.*

Hebrews 12:11 *No discipline is enjoyable while it is happening—it is painful! But afterward there will be a quiet harvest of right living for those who are trained in this way.*

James 1:3-4 *When your faith is tested, your endurance has a chance to grow. . . . For when your endurance is fully developed, you will be strong in character and ready for anything.*

When something is for our good, Christ's glory, and the building of his church, we should be happy to accept it, even though it involves suffering.

How do I stay close to God in times of suffering?

Psalm 22:24 *He has not ignored the suffering of the needy. He has not turned and walked away. He has listened to their cries for help.*

Recognize that God has not abandoned us in times of suffering.

Psalm 126:5-6 *Those who plant in tears will harvest with shouts of joy. They weep as they go to plant their seed, but they sing as they return with the harvest.*

Recognize that suffering is not forever. In the dark hours of the night of suffering it is hard to think of a morning of joy and gladness. But the tears of suffering are like seeds of joy.

Lamentations 3:32-33 *Though he brings grief, he also shows compassion according to the greatness of his unfailing love. For he does not enjoy hurting people or causing them sorrow.*

Recognize that God does not want to see us suffer. A loving God does not enjoy the disciplines of life that must come our way. But his compassionate love and care see us through our times of discipline and suffering.

Matthew 17:12 *Soon the Son of Man will also suffer at their hands.*

Luke 24:26 *Wasn't it clearly predicted by the prophets that the Messiah would have to suffer all these things before entering his time of glory?*

John 3:16 *God so loved the world that he gave his only Son, so that everyone who believes in him will not perish but have eternal life.*

Recognize that Jesus himself suffered for us. Christ suffered the agonies of the cross, which not only embraced incredible physical suffering but also the unthinkable suffering of bearing the sins of the world.

Romans 8:17-18 *Since we are his children, we will share his treasures—for everything God gives to his Son, Christ, is ours, too. But if we are to share his glory, we must also share his suffering. Yet what we suffer now is nothing compared to the glory he will give us later.*

Hebrews 2:18 *Since he himself has gone through suffering and temptation, he is able to help us when we are being tempted.*

PROMISE FROM GOD: 2 Corinthians 1:3-4 *All praise to the God and Father of our Lord Jesus Christ. He is the source of every mercy and the God who comforts us. He comforts us in all our troubles so that we can comfort others. When others are troubled, we will be able to give them the same comfort God has given us.*

TALKING

See WORDS

TEMPTATION

Does temptation ever come from God?

James 1:13 *God is never tempted to do wrong, and he never tempts anyone else either.*

Mark 7:15 *You are defiled by what you say and do!* Temptation originates not in the mind of God but within the heart of man.

James 1:2 *Dear brothers and sisters, whenever trouble comes your way, let it be an opportunity for joy.* Although God does not send temptation, he does delight in helping us grow stronger through it.

What makes temptation so alluring?

Genesis 3:6 *The fruit looked so fresh and delicious. . . .*
So she ate some.

Satan's favorite strategy is to make that which is sinful
appear to be desirable and good.

1 Kings 11:1-3 *Solomon loved many foreign women. . . .*
And sure enough, they led his heart away from the LORD.

Often temptation begins in seemingly harmless pleasure,
soon gets out of control, and progresses to full-blown
idolatry.

How can I avoid falling into temptation?

Genesis 39:12 *He ran from the house.*

The best strategy is to flee the situation.

Proverbs 1:10 *If sinners entice you, turn your back on them!*

Sometimes our greatest tempters are those we think are our
friends.

Matthew 6:13 *Don't let us yield to temptation.*

We should make our temptations a constant focus of prayer.

Titus 2:12 *We are instructed to turn from godless living*
and sinful pleasures.

Christian growth brings an increased awareness and
sensitivity to temptation in our lives.

PROMISE FROM GOD: 1 Corinthians
10:13 *Remember that the temptations that come into your*
life are no different from what others experience. And God is
faithful. He will keep the temptation from becoming so strong
that you can't stand up against it. When you are tempted, he
will show you a way out so that you will not give in to it.

THANKFULNESS

See BLESSINGS AND THANKS

TIME

See PRIORITIES

TIMING OF GOD

How was God's timing critical in Jesus' life?

John 7:30 *The leaders tried to arrest him; but no one laid a hand on him, because his time had not yet come.*

Romans 5:6 *When we were utterly helpless, Christ came at just the right time and died for us sinners.*

Galatians 4:4 *When the right time came, God sent his Son, born of a woman, subject to the law.*

Ephesians 1:10 *This is his plan: At the right time he will bring everything together under the authority of Christ—everything in heaven and on earth.*

1 Timothy 2:6 *He gave his life to purchase freedom for everyone.*
This is the message that God gave to the world at the proper time.

1 Timothy 6:15 *At the right time Christ will be revealed from heaven by the blessed and only almighty God, the King of kings and Lord of lords.*

God's plan for his Son and his people is ordered—everything occurs just at the proper time. God knows why this timing is important, and someday we will understand.

How can I trust God's timing in my life?

Exodus 6:1 *"Now you will see what I will do to Pharaoh,"
the LORD told Moses. "When he feels my powerful hand upon
him, he will let the people go. In fact, he will be so anxious to
get rid of them that he will force them to leave his land!"*

Exodus 7:3, 5 *I will cause Pharaoh to be stubborn so I
can multiply my miraculous signs and wonders in the land of
Egypt. When I show the Egyptians my power and force them
to let the Israelites go, they will realize that I am the LORD.*

Exodus 9:16 *I have let you live for this reason—that you
might see my power and that my fame might spread
throughout the earth.*

Exodus 11:9 *The LORD had told Moses, "Pharaoh will
not listen to you. But this will give me the opportunity to do
even more mighty miracles in the land of Egypt."*

Exodus 12:36 *The LORD caused the Egyptians to look
favorably on the Israelites, and they gave the Israelites
whatever they asked for. So, like a victorious army, they
plundered the Egyptians!*

John 11:1-6, 14-15, 21, 32, 43-45 *A man named
Lazarus was sick. He lived in Bethany with his sisters, Mary
and Martha. . . . So the two sisters sent a message to Jesus
telling him, "Lord, the one you love is very sick." But when
Jesus heard about it he said, "Lazarus's sickness will not end
in death. No, it is for the glory of God. I, the Son of God, will
receive glory from this." Although Jesus loved Martha, Mary,*

and Lazarus, he stayed where he was for the next two days and did not go to them. . . . Then he told [his disciples] plainly, "Lazarus is dead. And for your sake, I am glad I wasn't there, because this will give you another opportunity to believe in me. Come, let's go see him." . . . Martha said to Jesus, "Lord, if you had been here, my brother would not have died. . . . When Mary arrived and saw Jesus, she fell down at his feet and said, "Lord, if you had been here, my brother would not have died." . . . Then Jesus shouted, "Lazarus, come out!" And Lazarus came out, bound in graveclothes, his face wrapped in a headcloth. Jesus told them, "Unwrap him and let him go!" Many of the people who were with Mary believed in Jesus when they saw this happen.

Isaiah 25:1   *O LORD, I will honor and praise your name, for you are my God. You do such wonderful things! You planned them long ago, and now you have accomplished them.*

Habakkuk 2:3   *These things I plan won't happen right away. Slowly, steadily, surely, the time approaches when the vision will be fulfilled. If it seems slow, wait patiently, for it will surely take place. It will not be delayed.*

Romans 12:12   *Be glad for all God is planning for you. Be patient in trouble, and always be prayerful.*

Many times God will intervene in your life in a special way. Watch for those times, and then praise God that you can play a part, even if it is a small one, in the movement of God in this world.

How can I best wait for God's timing?

Psalm 31:5   *I entrust my spirit into your hand. Rescue me, LORD, for you are a faithful God.*

Psalm 59:9 *You are my strength; I wait for you to rescue me, for you, O God, are my place of safety.*

Psalm 69:13 *I keep right on praying to you, LORD, hoping this is the time you will show me favor. In your unfailing love, O God, answer my prayer with your sure salvation.*

Psalm 138:3 *When I pray, you answer me; you encourage me by giving me the strength I need.*

Isaiah 40:31 *Those who wait on the LORD will find new strength. They will fly high on wings like eagles. They will run and not grow weary. They will walk and not faint.*

With patience and alertness

PROMISE FROM GOD: Habakkuk 2:3 *These things I plan won't happen right away. Slowly, steadily, surely, the time approaches when the vision will be fulfilled. If it seems slow, wait patiently, for it will surely take place. It will not be delayed.*

TIRED

Why am I so tired?

Job 7:1-3 *Is this not the struggle of all humanity? A person's life is long and hard, like that of a hired hand, like a worker who longs for the day to end, like a servant waiting to be paid. I, too, have been assigned months of futility, long and weary nights of misery.*

The struggles of life are tiring because they are many and long.

Nehemiah 4:10 *The people of Judah began to complain that the workers were becoming tired. There was so much rubble to be moved that we could never get it done by ourselves.*

Too much work can drain us.

Proverbs 23:4 *Don't weary yourself trying to get rich. Why waste your time?*

We may be tired because we are striving for something that is not God's will.

2 Corinthians 5:2 *We grow weary in our present bodies, and we long for the day when we will put on our heavenly bodies like new clothing.*

We get tired because of the limitations of our present bodies.

1 Samuel 14:24 *The men of Israel were worn out that day, because Saul had made them take an oath, saying, "Let a curse fall on anyone who eats before evening—before I have full revenge on my enemies." So no one ate a thing all day.*

Not eating properly can make us tired.

John 4:6 *Jacob's well was there; and Jesus, tired from the long walk, sat wearily beside the well about noontime.*

Overworking or exercising too long will make us tired.

Ecclesiastes 12:12 *My child, be warned: There is no end of opinions ready to be expressed. Studying them can go on forever and become very exhausting!*

Not having the end in sight can make us tired.

Psalm 31:10 *I am dying from grief; my years are shortened by sadness. Misery has drained my strength; I am wasting away from within.*

Luke 22:45 *At last he stood up again and returned to the disciples, only to find them asleep, exhausted from grief.*
Grief can drain our strength.

Who can help me when I grow weary?

Isaiah 40:29-31 *He gives power to those who are tired and worn out; he offers strength to the weak. Even youths will become exhausted, and young men will give up. But those who wait on the LORD will find new strength. They will fly high on wings like eagles. They will run and not grow weary. They will walk and not faint.*

Isaiah 49:4 *I replied, "But my work all seems so useless! I have spent my strength for nothing and to no purpose at all. Yet I leave it all in the LORD's hand; I will trust God for my reward."*

Jeremiah 31:25 *I have given rest to the weary and joy to the sorrowing.*

Habakkuk 3:19 *The sovereign LORD is my strength! He will make me as surefooted as a deer and bring me safely over the mountains.*

Matthew 11:28 *Jesus said, "Come to me, all of you who are weary and carry heavy burdens, and I will give you rest."*

2 Corinthians 12:9 *Each time he said, "My gracious favor is all you need. My power works best in your weakness." So now I am glad to boast about my weaknesses, so that the power of Christ may work through me.*

Hebrews 12:3, 12 *Think about all he endured when sinful people did such terrible things to him, so that you don't become weary and give up. . . . Take a new grip with your tired hands and stand firm on your shaky legs.*

The Lord will give us renewed strength when we grow weary.

PROMISE FROM GOD: Isaiah 40:29-31
He gives power to those who are tired and worn out; he offers strength to the weak. Even youths will become exhausted, and young men will give up. But those who wait on the LORD will find new strength. They will fly high on wings like eagles. They will run and not grow weary. They will walk and not faint.

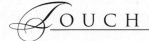

TOUCH

How did Jesus use physical touch during his time on earth?

Mark 10:16 *He took the children into his arms and placed his hands on their heads and blessed them.*

Luke 4:40 *As the sun went down that evening, people throughout the village brought sick family members to Jesus. No matter what their diseases were, the touch of his hand healed every one.*

Mark 5:28 *She thought to herself, "If I can just touch his clothing, I will be healed."*

John 20:27 *Then he said to Thomas, "Put your finger here and see my hands. Put your hand into the wound in my side. Don't be faithless any longer. Believe!"*

Jesus used touch to comfort, affirm, heal, bless, and encourage.

What are some of the purposes of physical touch?

Genesis 33:4 *Esau ran to meet him and embraced him affectionately and kissed him. Both of them were in tears.*

Genesis 45:15 *Joseph kissed each of his brothers and wept over them, and then they began talking freely with him.*

Luke 15:20 *He returned home to his father. And while he was still a long distance away, his father saw him coming. Filled with love and compassion, he ran to his son, embraced him, and kissed him.*

Greetings

Genesis 31:28, 55 *"Why didn't you let me kiss my daughters and grandchildren and tell them good-bye? You have acted very foolishly!" . . . Laban got up early the next morning, and he kissed his daughters and grandchildren and blessed them. Then he returned home.*

1 Samuel 20:41 *As soon as the boy was gone, David came out from where he had been hiding near the stone pile. Then David bowed to Jonathan with his face to the ground. Both of them were in tears as they embraced each other and said good-bye, especially David.*

Acts 20:37 *They wept aloud as they embraced him in farewell.*

Farewells

Luke 7:38 *She knelt behind him at his feet, weeping. Her tears fell on his feet, and she wiped them off with her hair. Then she kept kissing his feet and putting perfume on them.*

Thankfulness

Exodus 17:12 *Moses' arms finally became too tired to hold up the staff any longer. So Aaron and Hur found a stone for him to sit on. Then they stood on each side, holding up his hands until sunset.*

Acts 9:9 *His companions led him by the hand to Damascus. He remained there blind for three days. And all that time he went without food and water.*

Helping

Song of Songs 1:2 *Young Woman: "Kiss me again and again, for your love is sweeter than wine."*

Song of Songs 2:6 *His left hand is under my head, and his right hand embraces me.*

Intimacy

Acts 6:6 *These seven were presented to the apostles, who prayed for them as they laid their hands on them.*

Acts 8:17 *Peter and John laid their hands upon these believers, and they received the Holy Spirit.*

1 Timothy 4:14 *Do not neglect the spiritual gift you received through the prophecies spoken to you when the elders of the church laid their hands on you.*

Ministry

What are some of the dangers and abuses of physical touch?

Exodus 21:12 *Anyone who hits a person hard enough to cause death must be put to death.*

Job 31:21-22 *If my arm has abused an orphan because I thought I could get away with it, then let my shoulder be wrenched out of place! Let my arm be torn from its socket!*

Job 38:15 *The light disturbs the haunts of the wicked, and it stops the arm that is raised in violence.*

John 19:3 *"Hail! King of the Jews!" they mocked, and they hit him with their fists.*
Violence and physical abuse

Luke 22:47-48 *Even as he said this, a mob approached, led by Judas, one of his twelve disciples. Judas walked over to Jesus and greeted him with a kiss. But Jesus said, "Judas, how can you betray me, the Son of Man, with a kiss?"*
Deceitfulness of a kiss

Genesis 20:6 *"Yes, I know you are innocent," God replied. "That is why I kept you from sinning against me; I did not let you touch her."*

Leviticus 18:6 *You must never have sexual intercourse with a close relative, for I am the LORD.*

Deuteronomy 27:21 *Cursed is anyone who has sexual intercourse with an animal.*

Proverbs 6:29 *So it is with the man who sleeps with another man's wife. He who embraces her will not go unpunished.*

Romans 1:26-27 *That is why God abandoned them to their shameful desires. Even the women turned against the natural way to have sex and instead indulged in sex with each other. And the men, instead of having normal sexual relationships with women, burned with lust for each other. Men did shameful things with other men and, as a result, suffered within themselves the penalty they so richly deserved.*
Sexual abuse

PROMISE FROM GOD: **Job 5:19** *He will rescue you again and again so that no evil can touch you.*

TRADITIONS

Why are traditions important?

Exodus 12:14 *You must remember this day forever. Each year you will celebrate it as a special festival to the LORD.*

God endorses traditions, especially those that have spiritual significance. Traditions promote togetherness and help us remember all that God has done for us. The greatest inheritance you can provide for succeeding generations is a tradition that reminds them frequently of God's blessings and warnings.

Joel 1:3 *Tell your children about it in the years to come. Pass the awful story down from generation to generation.*

Joel tells of a horrible plague of locusts that had come to destroy the land. It is a sign of coming judgment at the hands of the Assyrians and Chaldeans. Joel tells his people to pass this awful story down from generation to generation, a tradition of sorts, to remind them to obey God and thus avoid his judgment.

When wonderful things happen, how can I pass them on to my children and grandchildren?

Esther 9:28 *These days would be remembered and kept from generation to generation and celebrated by every family.*

God had done wonderful things for the Jewish people through Esther, things so wonderful that they must not be forgotten for generations to come. Make it an annual tradition to share past blessings.

Are there dangers to look out for regarding traditions?

Deuteronomy 18:9 *When you arrive in the land the LORD your God is giving you, be very careful not to imitate the detestable customs of the nations living there.*

Matthew 15:2 *"Why do your disciples disobey our age-old traditions?" they demanded. "They ignore our tradition of ceremonial hand washing before they eat."*

Romans 4:11 *The circumcision ceremony was a sign that Abraham already had faith and that God had . . . declared him to be righteous—even before he was circumcised.*

Don't allow traditions or rituals to take your focus off Christ.

PROMISE FROM GOD: Deuteronomy 4:9 *But watch out! Be very careful never to forget what you have seen the LORD do for you. Do not let these things escape from your mind as long as you live! And be sure to pass them on to your children and grandchildren.*

TRUST

What does it mean to trust God?

Psalm 33:21 *In him our hearts rejoice, for we are trusting in his holy name.*

It means recognizing that God is trustworthy and then trusting him above all else.

Genesis 6:14, 17, 22 *"Make a boat. . . . I am about to cover the earth with a flood." . . . Noah did everything exactly as God had commanded him.*

Trusting God means obeying his commands even when we don't fully understand.

Psalm 112:1 *Happy are those who delight in doing what he commands.*

We can trust God enough to obey because his word is true and will bring happiness.

John 3:36 *All who believe in God's Son have eternal life.*

Trusting God means depending on Christ alone for salvation.

Galatians 2:16 *No one will ever be saved by obeying the law.*

Trusting Christ for salvation means ceasing to trust in our own efforts to be righteous.

1 Peter 1:8 *Though you do not see him, you trust him; and even now you are happy.*

Trusting God produces joy.

PROMISE FROM GOD: Isaiah 26:3 *You will keep in perfect peace all who trust in you, whose thoughts are fixed on you!*

UNITY

What is true unity?

John 10:16 *I have other sheep, too, that are not in this sheepfold. I must bring them also, and they will listen to my voice; and there will be one flock with one shepherd.*

Romans 12:4-5 *Just as our bodies have many parts and each part has a special function, so it is with Christ's body. We are all parts of his one body, and each of us has different work to do. And since we are all one body in Christ, we belong to each other, and each of us needs all the others.*

1 Corinthians 12:18-20 *God made our bodies with many parts, and he has put each part just where he wants it. What a strange thing a body would be if it had only one part! Yes, there are many parts, but only one body.*

Galatians 3:28 *There is no longer Jew or Gentile, slave or free, male or female. For you are all Christians—you are one in Christ Jesus.*

Unity is not the same as uniformity. We are all different, with unique gifts and personalities. But when we can celebrate and appreciate our differences to reach the common goal of serving our Lord, that is true unity.

Why is unity important?

Acts 2:42-43 *They joined with the other believers and devoted themselves to the apostles' teaching and fellowship, sharing in the Lord's Supper and in prayer. A deep sense of awe came over them all, and the apostles performed many miraculous signs and wonders.*

Romans 15:6 *All of you can join together with one voice, giving praise and glory to God, the Father of our Lord Jesus Christ.*

1 Corinthians 1:10 *Dear brothers and sisters, I appeal to you by the authority of the Lord Jesus Christ to stop arguing among yourselves. Let there be real harmony so there won't be divisions in the church. I plead with you to be of one mind, united in thought and purpose.*

Psalm 133:1 *How wonderful it is, how pleasant, when brothers live together in harmony!*
Unity brings a shared sense of purpose and devotion.

How do we achieve unity?

Romans 15:5 *May God, who gives this patience and encouragement, help you live in complete harmony with each other—each with the attitude of Christ Jesus toward the other.*
Through adopting a Christlike attitude

Ephesians 4:12-13 *Their responsibility is to equip God's people to do his work and build up the church, the body of Christ, until we come to such unity in our faith and knowledge of God's Son that we will be mature and full grown in the Lord, measuring up to the full stature of Christ.*
By exercising our God-given gifts

1 Peter 3:8 *All of you should be of one mind, full of sympathy toward each other, loving one another with tender hearts and humble minds.*
By sympathizing with each other

Ephesians 4:2-3 *Be humble and gentle. Be patient with each other, making allowance for each other's faults because of your love. Always keep yourselves united in the Holy Spirit, and bind yourselves together with peace.*
By being humble and gentle

Colossians 3:13-14 *You must make allowance for each other's faults and forgive the person who offends you. . . . Love is what binds us all together in perfect harmony.*
By loving and forgiving each other

PROMISE FROM GOD: Romans 15:6 *All of you can join together with one voice, giving praise and glory to God, the Father of our Lord Jesus Christ.*

VULNERABILITY

How do I keep myself from being vulnerable to harm?

Lamentations 1:8 *Jerusalem has sinned greatly, so she has been tossed away like a filthy rag. All who once honored her now despise her, for they have seen her stripped naked and humiliated. All she can do is groan and hide her face.*

Nahum 3:5 *"No wonder I am your enemy!" declares the LORD Almighty. "And now I will lift your skirts so all the earth will see your nakedness and shame."*

Shame and humiliation can be the direct consequences of disobedience to God.

Numbers 14:42 *Moses said, "Why are you now disobeying the LORD's orders to return to the wilderness? It won't work. Do not go into the land now. You will only be crushed by your enemies because the LORD is not with you."*

Deuteronomy 28:48 *You will serve your enemies whom the LORD will send against you. You will be left hungry, thirsty, naked, and lacking in everything. They will oppress you harshly until you are destroyed.*

We can keep ourselves from being vulnerable to harm by obeying God and staying within his plan and revealed will.

Ezra 8:22-23 *We had told the king, "Our God protects all those who worship him, but his fierce anger rages against those* who abandon him." *So we fasted and earnestly prayed that our God would take care of us, and he heard our prayer.*

If we pray to God for his protection and care, he will take care of us.

Nehemiah 4:13 *I placed armed guards behind the lowest parts of the wall in the exposed areas. I stationed the people to stand guard by families, armed with swords, spears, and bows.*

We can keep from being vulnerable by joining together with others and standing together against danger.

Revelation 16:15 *Take note: I will come as unexpectedly as a thief! Blessed are all who are watching for me, who keep their robes ready so they will not need to walk naked and ashamed.*

If we are fully prepared for Christ's coming, we will not be vulnerable to judgment when he comes.

Is God vulnerable in any way?

Isaiah 53:12 *I will give him the honors of one who is mighty and great, because he exposed himself to death. He was counted among those who were sinners. He bore the sins of many and interceded for sinners.*

God, in Christ, made himself vulnerable to abuse and death at the hands of evil people.

Matthew 4:1 *Jesus was led out into the wilderness by the Holy Spirit to be tempted there by the Devil.*

Jesus made himself vulnerable to temptation, but he resisted.

PROMISE FROM GOD: Romans 5:6 *When we were utterly helpless, Christ came at just the right time and died for us sinners.*

WAITING

See PATIENCE

WILL OF GOD

See GOD'S WILL AND
THE HAND OF GOD

WISDOM

How do I obtain wisdom?

Job 28:28 *The fear of the Lord is true wisdom; to forsake evil is real understanding.*

God gives wisdom to those who fear him and forsake evil.

1 John 2:27 *You have received the Holy Spirit, and he lives within you, so you don't need anyone to teach you what is true. For the Spirit teaches you all things, and what he teaches is true—it is not a lie. So continue in what he has taught you, and continue to live in Christ.*

Wisdom comes from having a relationship with God.

Proverbs 1:5-6 *Let those who are wise listen to these proverbs and become even wiser. And let those who understand receive guidance by exploring the depth of meaning in these proverbs, parables, wise sayings, and riddles.*

Obedience to God's Word—his commands, laws, and teachings—will make us wise.

Psalm 86:11 *Teach me your ways, O LORD, that I may live according to your truth! Grant me purity of heart, that I may honor you.*

James 1:5 *If you need wisdom—if you want to know what God wants you to do . . . ask him, and he will gladly tell you. He will not resent your asking.*

If you need wisdom, ask God, and he will give it.

Colossians 3:16 *Let the words of Christ, in all their richness, live in your hearts and make you wise. Use his words to teach and counsel each other.*

Listening to Christ's teachings and obeying his words will give wisdom.

Proverbs 8:12, 17 *I, Wisdom, live together with good judgment. I know where to discover knowledge and discernment. . . . I love all who love me. Those who search for me will surely find me.*

Those who seek wisdom are the ones who will find it.

PROMISE FROM GOD: Proverbs 3:5-6 *Trust in the LORD with all your heart; do not depend on your own understanding. Seek his will in all you do, and he will direct your paths.*

WORDS

What kinds of words should I speak?

Genesis 50:21 *He spoke very kindly to them, reassuring them.*

Speak kind words to others.

Psalm 50:23 *Giving thanks is a sacrifice that truly honors me.*

Romans 15:6 *All of you can join together with one voice, giving praise and glory to God, the Father of our Lord Jesus Christ.*
Speak words of thanks and praise to God.

Ephesians 4:29 *Let everything you say be good and helpful, so that your words will be an encouragement to those who hear them.*
Use words that build others up.

Proverbs 15:4 *Gentle words bring life and health.*

Proverbs 25:15 *Patience can persuade a prince, and soft speech can crush strong opposition.*
Speak to others with gentleness.

1 Peter 3:9 *Don't repay evil for evil. Don't retaliate when people say unkind things about you. Instead, pay them back with a blessing. That is what God wants you to do, and he will bless you for it.*
Use your words to bless even those who injure you.

Zechariah 8:16 *This is what you must do: Tell the truth to each other. Render verdicts in your courts that are just and that lead to peace.*
Speak truthfully.

What kinds of words should I avoid speaking?

Exodus 22:28 *Do not blaspheme God or curse anyone who rules over you.*
Never curse God or anyone in leadership over you.

Ecclesiastes 10:20 *Never make light of the king, even in your thoughts. And don't make fun of a rich man, either. A little bird may tell them what you have said.*
Don't make fun of those in leadership.

Psalm 34:12-13 *Do any of you want to live a life that is long and good? Then watch your tongue! Keep your lips from telling lies!*

Avoid saying anything that is deceptive or false.

Proverbs 18:8 *What dainty morsels rumors are—but they sink deep into one's heart.*

Avoid spreading gossip or slander about other people.

Proverbs 29:11 *A fool gives full vent to anger, but a wise person quietly holds it back.*

Avoid speaking in the heat of anger; you will usually regret it later.

James 4:11 *Don't speak evil against each other, my dear brothers and sisters. If you criticize each other and condemn each other, then you are criticizing and condemning God's law.*

Avoid criticizing other people.

PROMISE FROM GOD: Proverbs 10:11 *The words of the godly lead to life.*

WORK

I'm a stay-at-home mom. How can God be glorified in my work?

1 Corinthians 10:31 *Whatever you do, you must do all for the glory of God.*

I'm a working mother. What does God think about this?

Genesis 2:2, 15 *Having finished his task, God rested from all his work. . . . The LORD God placed the man in the Garden of Eden to tend and care for it.*

Our work is anchored in God's very character; part of being made in his image is sharing the industrious and creative aspects of his nature.

2 Thessalonians 3:8 *We worked hard day and night so that we would not be a burden to any of you.*

Christians are commanded to work hard at whatever they do.

Colossians 3:23 *Work hard and cheerfully at whatever you do, as though you were working for the Lord.*

The way we approach work is evidence of our relationship to Christ.

How can I balance work and my family?

Psalm 39:6 *All our busy rushing ends in nothing.*

Ecclesiastes 5:3 *Being too busy gives you nightmares.*

While we are called to work hard, we must make sure that our work doesn't so preoccupy us that we endanger our health, our relationships, or our time with God.

Acts 16:16 *She was a fortune-teller who earned a lot of money for her masters.*

We must make sure that we don't allow our work to compromise our values.

Exodus 16:23 *The LORD has appointed tomorrow as a day of rest.*

Mark 6:31 *Then Jesus said, "Let's get away from the crowds for a while and rest."*

There is a time to stop our work in order to rest, to celebrate, and to worship God.

Is it possible to work your way into heaven?

Ecclesiastes 2:11 *But as I looked at everything I had worked so hard to accomplish, it was all so meaningless.*

Although we are to work hard, work by itself does not bring ultimate fulfillment.

Ephesians 2:9 *Salvation is not a reward for the good things we have done.*

All our work and good deeds, no matter how impressive, will never save us.

PROMISES FROM GOD: Psalm 145:14 *The LORD helps the fallen and lifts up those bent beneath their loads.*

Philippians 1:6 *And I am sure that God, who began the good work within you, will continue his work until it is finally finished on that day when Christ Jesus comes back again.*

WORRY

When does worry become sin?

Matthew 13:22 *The thorny ground represents those who hear and accept the Good News, but all too quickly the message is crowded out by the cares of this life.*

Colossians 3:2 *Let heaven fill your thoughts. Do not think only about things down here on earth.*

Our worry over the concerns of life becomes sin when it prevents the Word of God from taking root in our lives.

Why do I worry so much? How can I worry less?

Psalm 55:4 *My heart is in anguish.*

Fear and anxiety are normal responses to threatening situations.

Exodus 14:13 *Moses told the people, "Don't be afraid. Just stand where you are and watch the LORD rescue you."*

We combat worry and anxiety by remembering and trusting God's promises.

Philippians 4:6 *Don't worry about anything; instead, pray about everything.*

We combat worry by placing our cares in Jesus' hands.

Psalm 62:6 *He alone is my rock and my salvation, my fortress where I will not be shaken.*

We find relief from worry in the promise of salvation.

Matthew 6:25 *Can all your worries add a single moment to your life?*

Our worries lose their grip on us as we focus on kingdom priorities.

PROMISE FROM GOD: 1 Peter 5:7 *Give all your worries and cares to God, for he cares about what happens to you.*

WORSHIP

How is worship integral to my relationship with God?

1 Chronicles 16:29 *Give to the LORD the glory he deserves! Bring your offering and come to worship him. Worship the LORD in all his holy splendor.*

Psalm 145:3 *Great is the LORD! He is most worthy of praise! His greatness is beyond discovery!*
Worship is the recognition of who God is and of who we are in relation to him.

Exodus 29:43 *I will meet the people of Israel there, and the Tabernacle will be sanctified by my glorious presence.*
God meets with his people in a powerful way when they worship him together.

Deuteronomy 31:11 *You must read this law to all the people of Israel when they assemble before the LORD your God at the place he chooses.*

Micah 4:2 *Come, let us go up to the mountain of the LORD, to the Temple of the God of Israel. There he will teach us his ways, so that we may obey him.*
Public, corporate worship gives God's people an important opportunity to hear his word proclaimed and learn about God and his ways.

Psalm 5:7 *Because of your unfailing love, I can enter your house; with deepest awe I will worship at your Temple.*

Isaiah 6:3 *In a great chorus they sang, "Holy, holy, holy is the LORD Almighty! The whole earth is filled with his glory!"*
Worship is a fitting response to God's holiness, power, and grace.

Revelation 4:9-11 *Whenever the living beings give glory and honor and thanks to the one sitting on the throne, the one who lives forever and ever, the twenty-four elders fall down and worship the one who lives forever and ever. And they lay their crowns before the throne and say, "You are worthy, O Lord our God, to receive glory and honor and power. For you created everything, and it is for your pleasure that they exist and were created."*

Our worship of God is a foretaste of heaven.

What should worship include?

Genesis 35:2-3 *Jacob told everyone in his household, "Destroy your idols, wash yourselves, and put on clean clothing. We are now going to Bethel, where I will build an altar to the God who answered my prayers when I was in distress. He has stayed with me wherever I have gone."*

Deuteronomy 11:16 *Do not let your heart turn away from the LORD to worship other gods.*

We must worship only God!

Exodus 3:5 *"Do not come any closer," God told him. "Take off your sandals, for you are standing on holy ground."*

When we enter God's presence in worship, we should recognize that we are standing on holy ground.

Psalm 35:18 *I will thank you in front of the entire congregation. I will praise you before all the people.*

Our worship should include praise and giving thanks to God for what he has done.

1 Chronicles 13:8 *David and all Israel were celebrating before God with all their might, singing and playing all kinds of musical instruments—lyres, harps, tambourines, cymbals, and trumpets.*

Worship can take the form of a joyous celebration with instruments of music.

Psalm 95:6 *Come, let us worship and bow down. Let us kneel before the LORD our maker.*

Kneeling and bowing are appropriate postures for worship.

Hebrews 12:28 *Since we are receiving a Kingdom that cannot be destroyed, let us be thankful and please God by worshiping him with holy fear and awe.*

Holy fear and awe should accompany thanksgiving in worship.

Amos 5:21 *I hate all your show and pretense—the hypocrisy of your religious festivals and solemn assemblies.*

Public worship is worse than useless if done without sincerity and the fruit of righteous living.

PROMISE FROM GOD: Philippians 2:9-11 *Because of this, God raised him up to the heights of heaven and gave him a name that is above every other name, so that at the name of Jesus every knee will bow, in heaven and on earth and under the earth, and every tongue will confess that Jesus Christ is Lord, to the glory of God the Father.*

WORTH / WORTHINESS

In what ways is God worthy?

Psalm 33:4 *The word of the LORD holds true, and everything he does is worthy of our trust.*

WORTH/WORTHINESS

Psalm 145:3 *Great is the LORD! He is most worthy of praise! His greatness is beyond discovery!*

Revelation 4:11 *You are worthy, O Lord our God, to receive glory and honor and power. For you created everything, and it is for your pleasure that they exist and were created.*

God is worthy of our praise, worship, and trust.

What am I worth—what is my value to God?

Deuteronomy 26:18 *The LORD has declared today that you are his people, his own special treasure, just as he promised, and that you must obey all his commands.*

Psalm 8:5 *You made us only a little lower than God, and you crowned us with glory and honor.*

Matthew 16:26 *How do you benefit if you gain the whole world but lose your own soul in the process? Is anything worth more than your soul?*

God made us in his own image, so he must value us highly! He also emphasizes how important our souls are to him.

What makes me worthy?

1 Corinthians 7:23 *God purchased you at a high price. Don't be enslaved by the world.*

I am worthy because God paid a high price for me.

Ephesians 1:4-5 *Long ago, even before he made the world, God loved us and chose us in Christ to be holy and without fault in his eyes. His unchanging plan has always been to adopt us into his own family by bringing us to himself through Jesus Christ.*

Before God made the world, he chose us to be born as his unique creations, holy and forgiven.

How can I keep my life focused on things of worth?

Psalm 119:37 *Turn my eyes from worthless things, and give me life through your word.*

Luke 10:42 *There is really only one thing worth being concerned about. Mary has discovered it—and I won't take it away from her.*

Acts 14:15 *We have come to bring you the Good News that you should turn from these worthless things to the living God, who made heaven and earth, the sea, and everything in them.*

Acts 20:24 *My life is worth nothing unless I use it for doing the work assigned me by the Lord Jesus—the work of telling others the Good News about God's wonderful kindness and love.*

2 Corinthians 3:5 *It is not that we think we can do anything of lasting value by ourselves. Our only power and success come from God.*

Philippians 3:8 *Yes, everything else is worthless when compared with the priceless gain of knowing Christ Jesus my Lord. I have discarded everything else, counting it all as garbage, so that I may have Christ.*

Philippians 4:8 *Dear brothers and sisters, let me say one more thing as I close this letter. Fix your thoughts on what is true and honorable and right. Think about things that are pure and lovely and admirable. Think about things that are excellent and worthy of praise.*

PROMISE FROM GOD: Psalm 8:5 *You made us only a little lower than God, and you crowned us with glory and honor.*

INDEX

INDEX